MARY SHELLEY'S
FRANKENSTEIN

MARY SHELLEY'S
FRANKENSTEIN

The Classic Tale of Terror Reborn on Film

KENNETH BRANAGH

With the Screenplay by STEPH LADY *and* FRANK DARABONT

Photographs by DAVID APPLEBY
Afterword and Notes by LEONARD WOLF
Edited by DIANA LANDAU

PAN BOOKS

London, Sydney and Auckland

First published 1994 by Newmarket Press, New York,
and simultaneously in Canada

First published in Great Britain 1994 by Pan Books
an imprint of Macmillan General Books
Cavaye Place London SW10 9PG
and Basingstoke

Associated companies throughout the world

ISBN 0 330 33706 8

1 3 5 7 9 8 6 4 2

A CIP catalogue record for this book is available from
the British Library

Printed and bound in Great Britain by
Bath Press Colour Books

Contents

Did I request thee, Maker, from my clay
To mould me man? Did I solicit thee
From darkness to promote me?—

John Milton, *Paradise Lost*
(Mary Shelley's epigraph to *Frankenstein*)

A Tale for All Time

by Kenneth Branagh

Since this film is *Mary Shelley's Frankenstein*, our intent was always to arrive at an interpretation that's more faithful than earlier versions to the spirit of her book. Many people associate the word "Frankenstein" with very entertaining but rather melodramatic black-and-white features that were rather camp, even when they first came out—though they could also be very frightening.

So in thinking about the script, I began by reading the novel, which I had never read before. I found it extremely compelling. Some critics claim that it is not necessarily a great book—though it has great things in it—but it is a great *idea*. It's a central defining myth of creation, one that has been around in stories ever since there have been stories.

There are many dramatic ideas in Frankenstein: for example, the prospect of creating life, of a man playing God; and the idea of the noble savage, the disadvantaged creature who through misfortune discovers wisdom and compassion in a way that arrogant and complacent man cannot.

Mary Shelley captured a version of this myth that seems to have gripped the popular imagination. It clearly *is* a great idea, and yet many elements of the story have still to be put on film. To date, most interpreters have seized on the notion of the madman creating a monster. Whereas the book seems to be about a man—a dangerously sane, dangerously focused man—creating another human being. One endowed with supernormal powers and yet no exposure to what is considered normal. The result is a thing, a creature, a person of tremendous danger.

The idea was to use as much of Mary Shelley as had not been seen on film before. Having our script stay closer to the novel also allowed us to take things out that earlier films had invented. It was an advantage, for instance, not having a hunchbacked assistant around, or indeed anyone who forces Victor Frankenstein to say things like "Throw the galvanic flux meter! Switch to level seven!" That territory has been brilliantly covered elsewhere.

The novel does have some storytelling issues that a film must address. It was, after all, the work of a very young writer who is sometimes confusingly inconsistent with the plot. Our screenplay therefore came up with some inventions and redirections. Perhaps the most abiding and astonishing thing is the novel's very unspecific evocation of the creation process: Shelley almost completely ignores the details. It is a stroke of brilliance, really, because it has allowed artists in other mediums to interpret that part of the story in many imaginative and exciting ways.

We thought a great deal about how we would handle that famous Creation sequence, and I hope the results will enhance a modern audience's appreciation of Shelley's great story.

⁓

Some people will see this film as part of a phenomenon—the revival of gothic horror—especially coming soon after *Bram Stoker's Dracula*. I don't know if that is true, but these are stories which seem to operate on a primal level. Tales told by a fireside on a dark and stormy night, tales that grip the imagination and immediately transport us, but which at the same time ask fundamental questions about our existence.

Perhaps their renewed popularity has to do with where we are at this end of the twentieth century, at the dawn of a potential communications revolution which threatens our sense of identity or our sense of control. So we grasp at stories that explore life's fundamental questions. And these gothic tales seem to satisfy a deep-seated fascination with the limits of human experience. They discuss what birth, life, and death mean—why we're here.

Maybe there aren't many stories—maybe there are only six or seven that get retold—but this is one of them, I have no doubt. This is one of the great tales.

And in some way, moviemakers now seem able to deal with such stories in a very different way, one that tries to connect with our experiences as directly as the tales themselves do, rather than just trying to scare people or create easy pathos.

It's a great horror story. It's a wonderful adventure yarn about a man who builds a monster and doesn't get away with it. But it's also a moralistic fable about parental responsibility, the defiance of God, and the dangers of interfering with nature. Both simple and profound. All human life—and death—is there in *Mary Shelley's Frankenstein*.

Kenneth Branagh and Robert De Niro in a studio photograph.
Preceding page: Prop photo of Victor's bloodstained journal.

Mary Shelley, Frankenstein's Creator

by Leonard Wolf

What terrified me will terrify others…

—Mary Shelley

Who was Mary Shelley, and how did she come to write *Frankenstein*?

Mary Shelley (1797–1851) was still a teenager when she wrote the world's most famous horror novel. It all began on a dark and stormy night in June 1816, when she and her lover, the poet Percy Shelley, were visiting Lord Byron at his home, the Villa Diodati, in Geneva. John Polidori, Byron's personal physician and sometime lover, was there, as was Claire Clairmont, Mary Shelley's stepsister, with whom the "mad, bad, and dangerous to know" Byron had had a brief affair.

At some point in the evening, Byron suggested that they should all write a ghost story. Though both Byron and Percy Shelley made a stab at doing the assignment, only Polidori and Mary Shelley actually produced anything substantial as a result of Byron's whimsical suggestion. Polidori wrote *The Vampyre* and thus achieved a place in history by introducing the vampire into English literature. The nineteen-year-old Mary Shelley gave us *Frankenstein*.

She was born August 30, 1797, the daughter of Mary Wollstonecraft Godwin and William Godwin, who in their daughter's words were "persons of distinguished literary celebrity." William Godwin, the author of *An Enquiry Concerning Political Justice*, was one of England's leading radical thinkers.

Her mother, Mary Wollstonecraft, was one of the most fascinating women in English literary history, leading a tempestuous life until she married Godwin four months after she became pregnant by him. Overcoming the handicaps of a poverty-stricken childhood and an alcoholic and abusive father, she managed to educate herself and, astonishingly for an Englishwoman of her day, became a self-supporting professional woman who, in 1792, published the still-important essay, "A Vindication of the Rights of Women."

Her heroic and dramatic life was marked by episodes of depression and two unhappy love relationships, the second with an American journalist named Gilbert Imlay, whose daughter, Fanny, she bore in 1794. Imlay, whom Mary met in France while she was gathering material for a book on the French Revolution, was perpetually unfaithful to her, prompting two unsuccessful suicide attempts once she was back in England.

Then Godwin came on the scene, and a very brief period of happily married life followed. It ended four months after their marriage, when she died of dreadful complications that set in as she was giving birth to Mary Shelley on August 30, 1797.

Incompetent to raise his daughter Mary and Fanny Imlay, Godwin married again four years after his wife's death. This woman, a widow named Mary Jane Clairmont, had two children of her own: Charles and Jane, who would later call herself Claire.

Mary Shelley tells us, "As a child I scribbled, and my favourite pastime during the hours given me for recreation was to 'write stories.'" Sent away

to Scotland, to "the blank and dreary northern shores of the Tay, near Dundee," she consoled herself with compositions,

the airy flights of my imagination....I did not make myself the heroine of my tales... [but]...I could people the hours with creations far more interesting to me at that age than my own sensations.

When Mary was seventeen, she returned from one of those Scottish sojourns to find that the already famous poet Percy Bysshe Shelley, twenty-two, was now one of her father's friends. Shelley, who was unhappily married, was immediately drawn to Godwin's intensely brilliant young daughter. The pensive, fair young woman and the mercurial poet spent hours sitting by her mother's gravesite, holding hands and talking of deep things, and the inevitable followed a few months later: on July 28, 1814, they ran off together.

They escaped to the Continent where, bizarrely enough, they were joined by Mary's stepsister, now calling herself Claire. Perhaps even then but certainly later, Claire became an albatross around Mary Shelley's neck, playing the role of the understanding "other woman" in the Shelley ménage. She and Percy Shelley took long walks and had long talks whenever Mary was indisposed. Evidence suggests that the relationship at some point went beyond hand-holding and verbal consolation.

Six weeks after Percy and Mary's flight, the Shelleys were back in England and Mary Shelley was pregnant. That baby, a girl, was born prematurely in February 1815 and died two weeks later. Within two months Mary was pregnant again. Her second child, William, was born in January 1816. Percy and Mary were not to be married until December 1816, just after the suicide of the unfortunate first Mrs. Shelley.

In the summer of that year, Mary and Percy, accompanied by the ubiquitous Claire, were in Geneva to be near the poet Byron, whose baby

Opposite page: Portrait of Mary Wollstonecraft Shelley, by Richard Rothwell, 1840. National Portrait Gallery, London. Below: Geneva as Mary Shelley would have known it, in an undated engraving. The Bettmann Archive.

Claire was carrying. Mary, in her introduction to the 1831 edition, describes how she came to write *Frankenstein*, telling us first that Percy had long been after her "to prove myself worthy of my parentage and enrol myself on the page of fame. He was forever inciting me to obtain literary reputation.…Still, I did nothing. Traveling, and the cares of a family, occupied my time."

Then she recounts what happened that summer in Geneva when Byron read pages of his epic poem *Childe Harold* to his friends. It was, Mary notes,

> a wet, ungenial summer, and incessant rain often confined us for days to the house. Some volumes of ghost stories translated from the German into French fell into our hands.…

It was on one of those nights that Byron had his great idea. Turning to his guests, who included Percy Shelley and Mary Shelley, Dr. Polidori, and possibly Claire, he declared, "We will each write a ghost story…and his proposition was acceded to."

Acceded to but not, in fact, carried out. Though Byron seems to have started some kind of story, only Mary Shelley and John Polidori actually fulfilled his fanciful assignment. Mary, as she put it, busied herself to think of a story:

> …a story to rival those which had excited us to this task. One which would speak to the mysterious fears of our nature and awaken thrilling horror—one to make the reader dread to look round, to curdle the blood, and quicken the beatings of the heart.

For a long time, the requisite inspiring moment eluded her. Then one night

> When I placed my head on my pillow, I did not sleep, nor could I be said to think. My imagination, unbidden, possessed and guided me, fitting the successive images that arose in my mind with a vividness far beyond the usual bounds of revery. I saw—with shut eyes but acute mental vision—I saw the pale student of the unhallowed arts kneeling beside the thing he had put together. I saw the hideous phantasm of a man stretched out, and, then, on the working of some powerful engine, show signs of life and stir with an uneasy, half-vital motion. Frightful it must be…

And frightful it was, has been, and is.

The novel begun that fateful summer was finished on April 17, 1817, and published on March 11, 1818. The reviews

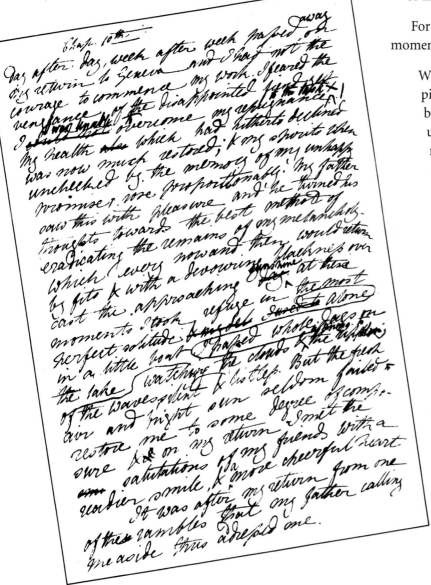

Opposite: First page of Frankenstein, *Vol. II, in Mary Shelley's own hand. Above: Percy Shelley's funeral pyre, painting by L. E. Fournier—an image eerily echoed by the ending of* Frankenstein. *The Bettmann Archive.*

were mixed. John Wilson Croker, in *The Quarterly Review*, said, "Our readers will guess from this summary, what a tissue of horrible and disgusting absurdity this work presents...." Croker added, "It cannot be denied that this is nonsense—but it is nonsense decked out with circumstances and clothed in language highly terrific...." He also admits that "*Frankenstein* has passages that appall the mind and make the flesh creep."

Sir Walter Scott, altogether a more astute critic, recognized that *Frankenstein* was

> An extraordinary tale, in which the author seems to us to disclose uncommon powers of poetic imagination....It is no slight merit in our eyes that the tale, though wild in incident, is written in plain and forcible English....Upon the whole, the work impresses us with a high idea of the author's original genius and happy power of expression [and we] congratulate our readers upon a novel which excites new reflections and untried sources of emotion.

If there was joy in the Shelley household on the appearance of *Frankenstein*, it was followed soon after by grief, for their surviving child, William, died in June 1818. In November of the same year, Mary gave birth to a second son, Percy Florence (named for the city of his birth).

Then, four years after the publication of *Frankenstein*, the thirty-year-old Percy Shelley was drowned at sea. It was a blow from which Mary never recovered. Though she continued to write and publish, nothing she produced after *Frankenstein* had its imaginative boldness.

When, in 1831, a new edition of *Frankenstein* was called for, she revised the novel of her youth, smoothing out the rawness of her primary vision and elevating its diction to the level of impeccable respectability. When she died on February 1, 1851, she was fifty-three years old. She was survived by her son Percy, and by what she had herself called her "hideous progeny"—the novel *Frankenstein*.

Frankenstein Reimagined

by Kenneth Branagh

Adapting a literary work—making it live in another medium in an interesting way, rather than just recording it—is something I've spent a lot of my limited film experience doing, particularly with Shakespeare. With *Mary Shelley's Frankenstein*, we wanted to follow the events of the novel as closely as practicable, to include as much of the story as possible, while tying everything to an overriding response to the material—that is, our interpretation of it.

For example, we wanted to use all the names correctly: in the 1931 film, Victor is called Henry Frankenstein, and they changed Henry's name to Victor. And we've brought in such characters as Mrs. Moritz and Justine, who were left out of earlier versions. So I hope we can justify the title *Mary Shelley's Frankenstein* by finding a legitimate marriage between a desire to use excellent things in the book that hadn't been seen before, and our contemporary response to the novel and its meaning.

Drawing by Chavalier for the 1831 edition of Frankenstein.

A Different Dr. Frankenstein

The first crucial departure for us was to render the character of Victor Frankenstein less of an hysteric—we believe Victor Frankenstein is not a mad scientist but a dangerously sane one. He is also a very romantic figure—there does seem to be much of Mary's beloved, Percy Bysshe Shelley, there. It was the dawn of the scientific age; Victor is someone ferociously interested in things of that nature. This was, as some have said, the last point in history when educated people could know virtually everything: have read every classic text, be aware of every experiment in physics, aware of medical developments, and so on. Victor, like Goethe, wanted to know more than he did, which was everything. Unlike Goethe, he discovers his limits tragically.

For me the lasting power of the story lay in its ability to dramatize a number of moral dilemmas. The most obvious one is whether brilliant men of science should interfere in the matters of life and death.

Today the newspapers are littered with such dilemmas—and they always bring up the word "Frankenstein"—for example, should parents choose the sex of their child? We can all see these developments taking place. It's now an imaginable step, to prevent people from dying. There's a place in the script where Victor says, "Listen, if we can replace one part of a person—a heart or a lung—then soon we will be able to replace every part. And if we can do that, we can design a life, a being that won't grow old, that won't sicken, a being that will be more intelligent than us, more civilized than us."

That element of Victor's philosophy is crucial.

This is a sane, cultured, civilized man, one whose ambition, as he sees it, is to be a benefactor of mankind. Predominantly we wanted to depict a man who was trying to do the right thing. We hope audiences today may find parallels with Victor today in some amazing scientist who might be an inch away from curing AIDS or cancer, and needs to make some difficult decisions. Without this kind of investigative bravery, perhaps there wouldn't have been some of the advances we've had in the last hundred years—an argument Mary Shelley makes on Victor's behalf in the book.

There are weaknesses in his character. He's driven by an unyielding resistance to the way the world seems to be ordered, a resistance to the apparently arbitrary reclamation of good and kind and important people. In Victor's case—and this is most resonant in the book—his mother, someone whom he clearly adores. In his anger and grief he resists the most irresistible fact of all—Death.

He has a relationship with God that is annoyed and irritated. He says to Henry, "We're talking about research and work that may mean that people who love each other can be together forever." Victor is also tremendously romantic. He feels that the apparent natural balance—we all arrive and know we are going to die—is not necessarily a perfect one. The romantic idea of souls being together forever—and in the wake of this scientific knowledge, *literally* together forever—is something that appeals strongly to his visionary instincts.

This version also portrays Victor as someone a little more physical, earthy as well as intellectual. Rather than a neurotic aesthete, he's sort of a renaissance man, someone who could be anything he wanted to be. Someone whose future the audience can care about. If he's a powerful figure, he has more to lose. And Victor is far from perfect. He is an obsessive overreacher who fails out of what he believes to be the noblest of motives.

It's been said that, in part, the story of Frankenstein is an expression of the frustration men feel at being unable to have children on their own, and alongside that goes revulsion at the birthing process. For example, after the operatic fervor of the creation process, as this film depicts it, with the camera swinging and swooping across the lab and a great sense of power being embodied by Victor Franken-

stein—the sarcophagus is suddenly thrown open and reveals this little stained burping thing which Victor is revolted by.

For anyone wishing to empathize with this character, perhaps the biggest difficulty of the book is the moment when Victor, having spent years researching and then building the Creature, is instantly repelled by it. It was one of the problems we felt we had to address: Why, after all this time, having seen what he was putting together, should he be so repelled and then be so frightened by it? We felt that if we did it exactly as the book does, it would be psychologically inconsistent with the Victor we were presenting.

The theme of parental abandonment is tremendously strong, and we tried to give Victor a moment when he is faced with what that means. "What have I done?" he says. Whether we find enough time to convince the audience that this shock has occurred—whether we believe that it would occur simply by seeing something that had been inanimate for a long time suddenly *be* there, and be so clearly and utterly dependent on him—

Theater of Anatomy, Cambridge University, 1818 aquatint by Combe. A model for the lecture hall in the film.

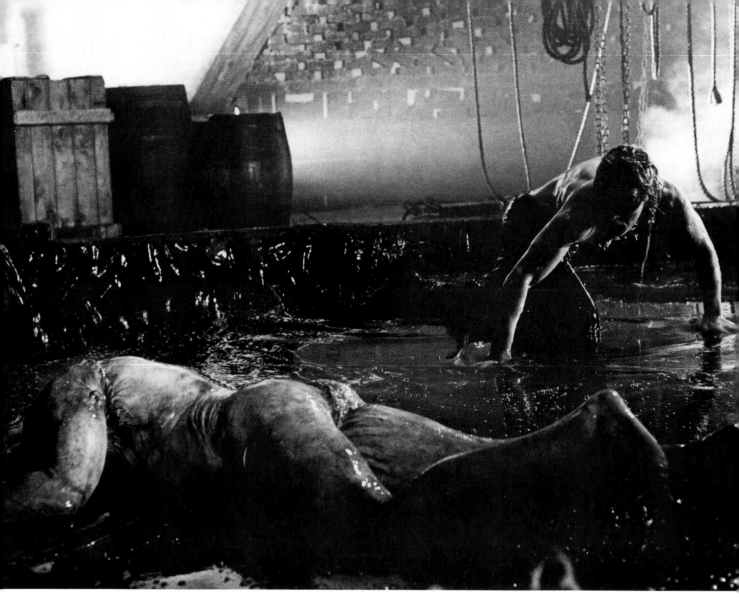

The Creature comes to life in the "birth sequence."

remains to be seen. There have certainly been distressing cases in modern times, where mothers have found it difficult to hold or care for their offspring immediately after birth. We took some of these examples as our cue.

Reimagining the Creation...

The image I had in my mind for the birth sequence is of a child being born to parents who then walk out of the delivery room and leave this bloodstained, fluid-covered thing to just crawl around on its own. The whole issue of pregnancy and the birthing process is such an emotive one, and creates such powerful feelings in people. We tried to make it explicit in that sequence. Indeed, the entire conception/creation process is full of explicitly sexual imagery.

The Creature, once alive, is wiped down, and banged on the back and made to cough out the remaining fluid, taught how to stand and walk—far away from the old image of the pre-dressed, lumbering villain rising up from the slab. The birth image itself is one of the most striking in the film. There is a tremendously thrilling, sexual, musical sequence leading up to a moment that is without music—you hear just the shlurping of the fluid and this Thing, grunting and groaning. Suddenly, from the feverishly idealized imagination of Victor Frankenstein we go to the reality of a living thing—created in this abortive fashion, alive in this utterly confused way, with a set of different parts—born to a dysfunctional father.

Literary scholars often look to Mary Shelley's own life for the sources of all this: the horror of her

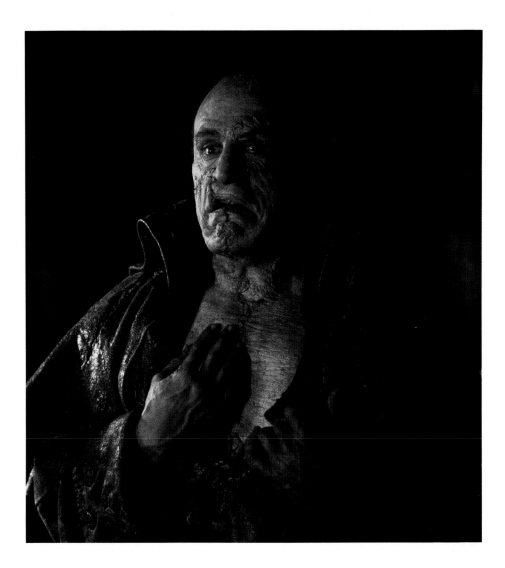

own birth with her mother dying as a result, and Mary's own children dying in infancy.

The lack of specific information that Shelley provides about the creation process leaves filmmakers free to imagine it all sorts of ways. It's fascinating in itself, and texturally it's a good thing to have in the middle of a story like this—this rhythm of the first section leading up to this climax of creation. In the earlier Frankenstein films, of course, you had that great gothic laboratory and the body being hauled up into the storm…It creates the sense of an epic struggle. Not unlike making a film, in fact. I sometimes feel there are uneasy parallels between Victor's obsessive desire to create his monster and what we've done in making a film of this size and scale. There is something compelling about watching a person in the grip of an obsession. People clearly enjoy watching other people go mad.

There is also a voyeuristic thrill to be had from watching the creation sequence. We feel as though we're behind closed doors. It's a secret. I hope the lonely and dangerous quality of this is something audiences will respond to.

…And the Creature

In portraying Frankenstein's Creature, we had the fundamental challenge of bringing to life in a different way a character that has already become universally familiar in another form. It began with certain decisions about the script—for example, that the Creature would learn to express himself eloquently, as he does in the book, rather than merely grunt. And of course Robert De Niro himself brought a great deal to the role.

Most people, let's face it, are really only aware of the Creature through comic books or the Munsters or the Addams Family. I think that to over-come such preconceptions, we had to cast an actor of power and stature. There should be something in the very casting, the very mention of the person's name, that would intrigue people as to how this great actor would interpret this classic screen role.

It was critical to conceive of a look for this Creature—through the combination of brilliant make-up and Robert's performance—that would be very different from Boris Karloff's memorable portrayal. It had to be striking and scary, yet allow Robert De Niro's face and expressions to be very clearly read through the make-up. All the prosthetic details, while powerful in themselves, are really just supporting the internal performance. We wanted to show also, through the make-up, that the Creature, though patched together from a collection of peo-ple, is illuminated by a confused but significant intelligence.

We took as a departure point the ice cave scene

in the book, where the Creature speaks so eloquently and articulately—using this to banish all comparison with the much less articulate Creature of earlier movies. (In the book, he and Frankenstein actually use a hut on the glacier, which we changed to a cave.) And again at the end, when speaking to Wal-ton, the Creature reveals a level of sophistication, at-tained through the course of his education in the book, that we felt was important to achieve.

In the ice cave scene the Creature faces Victor Frankenstein with the questions that any such being might ask: What were you doing? What am I made of? Did you ever consider the consequences of your actions? You gave me emotions, you didn't tell me how to use them. Do I have a soul or is that a part you left out? The "son" questioning his father about being abandoned. That's certainly the meat of the role for an actor like De Niro, and he takes it with tremendous relish.

Another early decision was to not make the

Creature an eight-foot tall giant as he is in the book. It should be clear that, for all the horror of his appearance, he is not in fact a monster, but a man. We wanted Robert, a man of medium height, to be neither smaller nor bigger than he is. We imply that the process of his creation endowed him with great physical strength, and perhaps an impression of a certain massiveness—but the idea of his being a giant has been seen too many times. It can also suggest the wrong sorts of comic possibilities, to do with his sexual longings and so on, which might be distracting. Mel Brooks's *Young Frankenstein* was such a brilliant parody that we wanted—without losing all humor in the film—to stay far away from "size gags."

The Creature's rage is the product of clearly articulated confusions about where he's come from and what he's made of. It's not simply the violence of a great big tall Thing. We wanted him to be much more like an ordinary man. But one without a name or an identity.

We wanted to concentrate a lot on De Niro's eyes—he has wonderful eyes—on trying to find the soul inside this collection of cuts and bruises and brain. That's what we want the audience to follow. There's a very strong image in Shelley's book of the Creature peering out between the boards of a pigsty, when he's crouched down and spying on the family. We reproduced that exactly, this image of the eyes as

windows of his soul.

We felt that the physical silhouette of the Creature, abetted by his costumes, had to have a kind of mythic power. Something that conjured up images of Japanese warriors, or monks—that sort of dignified, noble, powerful type who represents something of what the Creature has achieved by the end of his very unsentimental education. An innocent, he learns very quickly that because of how he looks, he'll be rejected by mankind. As he says, "I think and speak and know the ways of man." We wanted him to have the tone of a philosopher, someone who's found a strange peace even if he still is tormented and frustrated by not having the companionship that humans most often need to be happy.

It was the interior, the heart and soul of the Creature, that De Niro and I were most concerned with, and the exterior had to support that. We always thought of him as a naturally gentle soul whose rage is produced when he's crossed by Frankenstein. He achieves articulacy very early on. He's a swift learner, not lumbering or slow, and not without humor. It may be confusing to some people who like their monsters a bit more "monstery." The story and the Creature in this performance remain frightening and horrific, but we wanted at all times to sympathize with him or at least understand him.

Insofar as he is a man, he embodies both the

good and evil in man and inherits the doubts and worries and concerns all human beings have. We see a child grow up before us and we choose to dramatize those moments when this loss of innocence occurs.

The Family Frankenstein

The film, like the novel, depicts the Frankenstein household as a warm and loving one, something other films haven't chosen to focus on. Victor's background is very well-adjusted, full of warmth and sunshine, loving, kind, and indeed representative of something many people would be frightened of risking in the way he does.

We also looked back at the Shelleys' own lives to try to make the family relationships in the story as firmly grounded as possible. We read a lot about Mary Shelley's own mother and father, and the cir-cumstances of her and Percy's elopement, and the intensity of those relationships. It was a very romantic family and also very tough, all of them tremendously courageous.

We improvised in rehearsal. We resisted as much as possible any sense of "period" archness in the dialogue. The supporting characters have often been caricatures; we wanted to give more credit to the people around Victor Frankenstein.

We make a good deal of the mother's death, because I think Victor feels on a very simple level that it's a waste, a waste of such a woman. Not just a mother, but a woman of such qualities, such generosity, kindness—a shining example of what a good person might be. Witty, funny. It seems so arbitrary that she should be taken. Where is the justice in all this? What possible purpose can it serve?

A Love of Equals

Victor has a particular example of what he wishes to protect from the arbitrariness of fate—his loving relationship with Elizabeth, though he risks it in the very act of trying to protect it. As we've created it, this relationship is of intensity and magnitude, one where the two equal partners are brought up together as brother and sister, and have all the joy of that, and then miraculously find themselves attracted to each other in a full-blown adult way.

There is a quality of certainty about it, of cosmic "rightness," that this is a love where it's the right man and the right woman. There are no other people or games-playing or coquettishness; it's not even an issue. It's perfect, it was meant to be. They can make each other laugh, stimulate each other intellectually, and find each other physically attractive. It's a passionate love affair that the audience should want to identify with. Part of Victor's obsession is a fierce desire to protect that.

He deceives himself into believing that his work will be a finite thing, that he will get this over with and then come home. It's one more expression of the extraordinary vanity that men can have in these situations, their powers of self-deception. But he truly loves Elizabeth and she him, and in a way that the audience will find invigorating and uplifting. They both have a lot to lose. It's the sort of dilem-

ma that anyone can experience, pumped up to a very high level and very compelling.

The film *Dead Again*, as people have pointed out, also looked at that notion of a great love across time, that the right souls will find each other. I think people are tremendously seduced by that idea. It's present in the Shelley novel, but again only in the conventional sense in which such relationships could be presented: the woman at home, doing little, depending on social class and status; the man off working and sending back his devotional verse in letters, and worshiping her. But it's an unequal relationship. We couldn't be strictly authentic to the period, because I wanted to say at every stage: These two people are equal. This woman is possessed of as large an intelligence, as large a capacity for compassion and understanding as he is.

Elizabeth's response to the family tragedies is much different than his, though. She isn't driven in the same way as Victor. She's obsessed about her family, is someone who understands the value of what it can mean to be head of a household, and indeed wants to replace the great gap caused by the loss of his mother. She's someone who has a capacity to enjoy, to live in the present, to appreciate the small details of life. And she knows that to be that way is not to somehow be less of a person, which is Victor's and many men's tragedy. Just because you can't climb an enormous mountain doesn't mean that your life is without meaning. Elizabeth has the ability to accept things as they are, not live in some mythical future that people like Victor create.

In some strange way they complement each other. She allows him to go off, because that's what he needs to do. But it's not what she needs—she wants to stay at home. Every choice she makes is not a reactive decision but a decision by someone who has her own mind. It's shown in subtle ways but in ways that will be seen by everyone. Her character and their relationship are among the things we felt most strongly about in the film.

We felt it was crucial in a modern movie—especially of a novel by a great woman writer and the daughter of a very important feminist—to make sure that she is represented by someone who isn't just a "love interest." It's not an attempt to be politically correct. It's just very much more interesting, and more accurate about the current evolutionary state of the relations between men and women. We're also telling a story, a story where the narrative power is immense, and so I hope everything I'm talking about will be done in such as way as to be simply part of that story, and subtly enriching it as we go. We need to be thrilled by what happens next, and along the way hopefully be moved and affected by the romantic subplot.

The Erotic Edge Of Terror

Certainly there is something about the joining of romance and terror that's interesting and very effective cinematically. Human relationships seem to develop and deepen not in some sort of gentle, even gradient but as a result of traumatic shocks: divorce or bereavement or terrible situations that often force people to talk to each other. Something suddenly applies a flamethrower to chilly surfaces. So the fear of terrible events, or the actual execution of them, can a very effective means of compressing dramatically the journey of a relationship.

In this one we have Victor and Elizabeth truly growing up in the course of two hours, and I think that that can happen when tragedy enters into peoples' lives in a major way. It forces them to think about what is meaningful. When Elizabeth and the sick Victor reunite in his garret in the wake of the Creature's birth, they do so with renewed vigor and intensity and depth. And, loving each other that much, the idea of losing each other becomes that much more painful.

The wedding night scene, where the final not-quite-consummation of Victor and Elizabeth's love takes place, is further charged by the lurking terror outside, and in the back of Victor's mind. It's also sharpened by the knowledge that after this night of

love he will tell her what he's done. All this brings a sort of strange erotic thrill.

There is also a faintly incestuous side of the relationship which feels very right in relation to Mary Shelley and some of the events in her life. [See the preceding biographical note.]

Another moment with very strange, erotic, and no doubt grotesque overtones is the sequence in the film when Victor returns to the mansion and re-creates Elizabeth and then dances with her. Dancing has been important all the way through the picture—it's part of the ritual of romance, a social expression of physical attraction, celebratory and tactile and intoxicating, akin to making love. It's a thrilling embodiment of a romantic idea. And this final dance is, I think, profoundly moving, as well as a grotesque perversion of their extraordinary love. The sequence is our most radical departure from Shelley's novel, but one of the most haunting images in the film.

Also, the introduction of Elizabeth as the Crea-turess sets up a kind of sexual competition between Victor and the Creature. I think Mary Shelley was titillated in some way by the notion of the Creature and sex. When it occurs in the book that the Crea-ture wants a friend, at first it's dressed up nobly in the idea of companionship—but she also makes clear it's sexual. And Victor Frankenstein sees it. He realizes that this could lead to a whole tribe of these things. He's worried that the Creature will have sex.

We haven't played it out particularly, but it is clear at the end that she might be better off with the Creature than she would be with Victor. It is weird to imagine these two making love, or even Victor and the "new" Elizabeth—an incredible violation has taken place which contains great power to shock.

An Epic Fairy Tale

The dancing and the music and other elements of the film all fit into a particular style. We intended an epic sweep that takes us right outside ourselves. The subject matter, to begin with, is larger than life.

People encounter monsters, and the monsters are part of a bigger landscape, Switzerland itself, with huge mountains and evidence of the power of nature. We've made a lot of the sets oversize and played to the dynamic of small people against enormous forces, natural and manmade.

I had various images in mind, Hansel and Gretel figures going off into the dark woods—of little men screaming against the size of things, the scheme of things. The visual style of the film resembles a gothic fairy tale where we could be extreme.

We chose to represent the Frankenstein household, for example, as a bright, colorful house with huge rooms and lots of sunshine and light, and we took license with color. The family spends a lot of time in the huge blue ballroom, which has a magical quality and gothic size, but no real relationship to any particular architecture of the time—while not being so extremely at variance with the period as to distract.

In this visually heightened world, we wanted to have strong contrasts. When Victor goes to Ingolstadt, it looks as grimy and tough and real and disease-ridden as cities could be at that time. It's meant to be a striking contrast to Geneva. Victor comes from the light and moves into the dark. He goes back to the sunshine of the Frankenstein mansion afterward but it begins to be tainted by that moment when he shook hands with the Devil.

In general, fidelity to the period seemed less important than getting the psychological and emotional elements of the story right, and its relevance to our own scientific age, which are so compelling. Once a film becomes an authentic period rendition, then you have to pay much closer attention to period manners than for me seems relevant to this tale. That's a different kind of picture: I wanted this to be passionate and raw, sexy and fullblooded, and yet to be dressed as a fairy tale, a fairy tale where we are scared, where people die and have their heads chopped off.

The approach was, in a sense, part of an ongoing attitude to period that we've developed, about how to tell a story set in historical times. Where are the connections between now and what's meaningful about that story? The idea is to create an *impression* of a period, if it is more useful to the story than a specific and authentic reconstruction.

Though I adored *The Age of Innocence* for its meticulous attention to detail and evocation of period, that style wouldn't have been right for *Frankenstein*. It was Edith Wharton's technique to build up all those heavily detailed layers, whereas it's not Mary Shelley's at all. She uses a much broader brush. She was writing, as she says, a story "to quicken the pulse, curdle the blood, and quicken the beatings of the heart…" I wanted to do that as well.

There are some images that may suggest the German Expressionist style—tricks of perspective and looming shadows and the fairy-tale quality some of those films had.

I'm sure the style is influenced here and there by many different films. But I mostly used other pictures or styles as a means of conveying to colleagues what I *didn't* want.

A Tale Within a Tale

For the script we borrowed from Shelley the storytelling device of a tale within a tale. In the Arctic scenes that bracket the main action, Walton narrates to us what was told to him by Victor Frankenstein. Then, in the middle of Victor's tale, the Creature tells his. Like nesting boxes or a Fabergé egg.

Walton is very much a mirror image of Victor; he's another obsessive man at the beginning of his quest. Will this tale persuade him not to pursue it? Victor says to him: "Do you share my madness?"

And at the end, when they watch the bier drift off in the mist, Grigori, the first mate, who has been voicing the crew's mutinous disapproval of Captain Walton's obsession, says: "Where to now, Captain?" Walton says, "Home."

The sequence on the ice at the end has an elegiac quality, something very otherworldly about it. A culmination with wonderful Shelleyan images of fire and ice. We use a line at the end of the screenplay's screen directions which is the last line in the novel. As Walton watches from the deck of the ship, the Creature is soon "borne away by the waves and lost in darkness and distance." It's very mysterious and haunting.

And in the middle of the story comes the other crucial scene which takes place on the ice, when the Creature confronts Victor on the glacier. It's the central scene in the book, yet one that has strangely been avoided in every Frankenstein movie.

I wanted to make as many connections as I could between the entertaining surface and the underlying themes in the story. I wanted a film that people would be thrilled by, and also go out thinking, "What would *we* do?" There are great departure points for intelligent and lively debate. Not that that's necessarily required from a movie, but it's a wonderful thing when it happens. The richness of Mary Shelley's novel certainly encouraged us to stretch ourselves as artists, even though we know the interpretation of a genuine classic can never be definitive.

I hope Mary Shelley would at least approve of the attempt.

The Screenplay

"I busied myself to think of a story…which would speak to the mysterious fears of our nature and awaken thrilling horror—one to make the reader dread to look around, to curdle the blood, and quicken the beatings of the heart."

—*Mary Shelley*

Titles unfold in blackness…

V.O. (*as Mary Shelley*)
"I busied myself to think of a story which would
speak to the mysterious fears of our nature and
awaken thrilling horror…one to make the reader
afraid to look around, to curdle the blood and
quicken the beating heart."

Overall, the effect is mournful and haunting,
elegant and serene. As the credits end, the
following legend rises slowly up the screen:

LEGEND:

*The dawn of the nineteenth century. A world on the
brink of revolutionary change.*

Alongside political and social upheaval, scientific advances that would profoundly change the lives of all.

The lust for knowledge had never been greater. Among the pioneers: Captain Robert Walton, an explorer, obsessed with reaching the North Pole.

As the prize drew closer, his voyage would uncover a story to strike terror in the hearts of all who venture into the unknown....

SUPERTITLE:
The Arctic Sea, 1794

Merciless arctic winds whip the sea into a frenzy of 30-foot swells. A mist envelops the entire scene. The prow of a three-masted ship rises massively before us, looming from the darkness and chaos. It crashes upward through a swell and slams back down again, plunging nose-first into the trough. The sails on the forward mast are still deployed. It's insane; in this weather they should be stowed (as is already the case with masts two and three).

Hurtling toward us. Rising and falling. Thundering through the swells. And as she sweeps past camera within a seeming hair's breadth, we pan with the ship and find ourselves…

ON THE SHIP
Night

…aboard the *Alexander Nevsky*, along for the ride, whether we like it or not. There are men all around us, dark screaming figures glimpsed and half-glimpsed, heavy oilskin clothes flapping in the gale.

We track amongst them to find the Bosun (Mick) at the mizzenmast, finishing our shot on…a wild-eyed, bearded man, clutching the wheel in a white-knuckled death grip: Walton, captain of the *Nevsky*.

GRIGORI
Please, Captain, we have to drop the sails!

Walton moves off from the wheel, yelling at the Bosun.

WALTON
Take the wheel! Come on!

We move in front of and behind Walton as he moves up the deck and joins Grigori at the mainmast. Walton, Grigori, and all the other crewmen attack a guy-rope with primal fury.

Suddenly, a chilling cry from the bow of the ship.

LOOKOUT (O.S.)
Captain!!! We've hit the ice, we've hit the ice!

Walton and the others spin to look as the mist clears momentarily.

LOOKOUT
Iceberg ahead!

What they see is an iceberg rising massively and unexpectedly in the foreground, like a ghostly white mountain. They are heading straight for it and the rapidly appearing pack ice beyond.

Track in on Walton and the crew, frozen in breathless horror. The iceberg is almost upon them.

WALTON
Hard to starboard!

The Bosun and Joseph turn to make their way towards the wheel, but at that moment:

Smash! The ship lurches onto her port side as she hits the iceberg at the front. All the men are thrown onto the port side and turn to stare up at the iceberg as it rises up beside them. The ship ramming herself deeper into the ice.

Smack! And then the ship lurches again, this time over onto her starboard side and all the men are thrown across the ship.

Smash!! The prow slams into the pack ice up ahead of them.

Various quick-cut angles show men sliding sideways, tumbling, screaming. Everyone thrown forward. Walton and Grigori are thrown towards the front of the ship. They turn and look up to see the main topmast snap and begin to topple.

The topmast slams massively to the deck, knocking a crewman over the starboard side.

CREWMAN
Help!

WALTON
Hold on, man!

GRIGORI
Hold on!

Walton and Grigori race to the starboard rail and

34

look over the side to see the crewman crushed by the ice, and they then see a massive ice floe jamming itself up against the *Nevsky*. She is rapidly being caught in a net of ice.

Crunch!! The ice hits the starboard side.

Utter panic, mortal terror. The noise is terrifying as the stern is also enclosed with a crash. The *Nevsky* is completely locked in ice.

Grigori turns away in disgust and joins the rest of the crew, leaving Walton alone to look around him in sheer frustration.

Smash cut to:

ARCTIC ICE, THE *NEVSKY*
Twilight

Deafening silence. A glittering wasteland of ice. No signs of life. Slow pan reveals a distant ship frozen in the ice.

In low angle from the ice we see the crew working desperately with axes and picks to free the ship from the ice. They are near total exhaustion.

Nearby, a pack of dogs, huskies and malamutes, huddles in the snow. Walton checks the dogs and then moves on to check the crew as Grigori joins him.

WALTON
Put your backs into it, men.

GRIGORI
Captain, this is useless. The ice stretches for miles.

WALTON (*determined*)
What do you suggest, that we lay down and die?

GRIGORI
The men are exhausted. They can't go on, man.

WALTON
I tell you, I have not come this far to give up now. (*beat*) They knew the risks when they signed on. We'll chop our way to the North Pole if we have to.

GRIGORI
Then you run the risk of mutiny, Captain.

Walton stops and faces him.

WALTON
Did you say mutiny?

GRIGORI
Yes, I did, sir.

WALTON
We proceed north as planned.

Walton walks away and Grigori calls after him.

GRIGORI
At the cost of how many more lives?

WALTON (*stops and turns*)
As many as it takes.

As he turns to move on he is stoppped by a long, chilling howl. The lead husky rises to its feet, hackles up, howling and snarling at some unseen thing in the distance. All the huskies tied to the ship strain at their leashes.

GRIGORI (*terse, low*)
There's something out there.

WALTON (*to himself*)
What's out there?

The crew grab their weapons and then run to join their Captain.

They stare into the mist, seeing nothing. And then they see it:

An unearthly apparition looms eerily from the mist, freezing the crewmen's blood in their veins. They look on for what seems a heart-stopping eternity.

The Young Sailor aims a rifle.

Unbelievably, it's a man—Victor Frankenstein. He is dragging a sled. At the rear of the sled stand two poles over which is slung a huge billowing greatcoat, making the sled, as it looms out of the mist, look like a giant and sinister bat. As the sled gets nearer we notice that also tacked to the poles and dangling in the wind is the livid carrion of dead dogs: this, we gather, is the man's traveling larder.

Though exhausted, the man is fiercely determined. He stops in front of Walton, taking off his hood.

VICTOR
Who is your captain?

WALTON
I am. Who the devil are you?

About two o'clock the mist cleared away, and we beheld, stretched out in every direction, vast and irregular plains of ice, which seemed to have no end. Some of my comrades groaned, and my own mind began to grow watchful with anxious thoughts, when a strange sight suddenly attracted our attention, and diverted our solicitude from our own situation. We perceived a low carriage, fixed on a ledge and drawn by dogs, pass on towards the north, at the distance of half a mile: a being which had the shape of a man, but apparently of gigantic stature, sat in the sledge, and guided the dogs. We watched the rapid progress of the traveller with our telescopes, until he was lost among the distant inequalities of the ice.

Excerpts are from the
1818 edition of Frankenstein.

VICTOR
I haven't got time to talk. Bring your men and your weapons, and follow me. *(beat)* Now!

The men begin to follow him.

WALTON *(snapping)*
Stay where you are. I give the orders here.

All the huskies break free and hurl themselves snarling and barking into the mist.

WALTON
Get the dogs. Get them.

VICTOR
Leave them. They're already dead.

An inhuman howl rises from the mist. Fierce barking yielding to shrill squeals.

Cut to:

Another part of the ice floe. A dog jumps up high as if to attack something, the jaws moving fast towards camera. Close on what looks like an immense arm moving in slow motion through the mist. The screen is a blur of sound and confusion as one dog after another attacks and is throttled, smashed to the ice, or dismembered.

Back to the crew: they are filled with terror at the sound of the dogs' death-screams.

VICTOR *(to himself)*
He's out there.

Another inhuman howl in the mist.

WALTON
Get back to the ship. To the ship *now!*

The crew hurries to the safety of the ship.

ANOTHER PART OF THE ICE FLOE
Twilight

Close on a huge hand: thickly veined, yellow skin, resting on a rock in the foreground. Something, punching the air with rasps of breath, is watching the crew scatter back to the *Nevsky.*

Cut to:

The crew crowd around Grigori as he makes his way along the deck.

DAVE
It's a bloody animal.

MORRELL
Bears don't kill like that. Nothing does.

JENKINS
Maybe it wants the one with the Captain…

DAVE
…or it wants the Captain…

JENKINS
It's the devil come for the Captain.

Cut to:

INTERIOR OF WALTON'S CABIN
Twilight

VICTOR *(exasperated)*
For the last time, I made my way from St. Petersburg to Archangel on foot; from there I took a whaling ship north. When we hit the ice I used the dogs…

An inhuman howl from outside the ship. The two men exchange looks.

 Cut to ship's crew huddled together in fear on the deck.

JENKINS
(begins to recite a prayer)
"Yea, though I walk through the valley of the shadow of death…"

Cut back to cabin.

WALTON
What's out there?

ICE FLOE
Twilight

POV of something pounding across the ice, with the *Nevsky* in its sights. Short, powerful steaming jets of the Thing's breath are punched out before the camera. Whatever this Thing is, it's terrifyingly powerful.

Back to Walton's cabin: Victor rushes to the porthole. He peers out.

VICTOR
I've been chasing him for a month. I have to finish it.

Walton moves in beside Victor and grabs him, turns him.

WALTON *(threatening)*
Listen to me. I've spent six years planning this. My entire fortune. I will not be stopped by you or by some phantom.

VICTOR *(steely)*
Do you share my madness?

WALTON *(intense)*
No, not madness.

VICTOR
What, then?

WALTON
There is a passage to the North Pole. And I will find it!

VICTOR
At the cost of your own life and the lives of your crew?

WALTON
Lives come and go. If we succeed, our names will live on for ever. I will be hailed as the benefactor of our species.

VICTOR
You're wrong. I of all men know that.

WALTON
Who are you?

VICTOR *(tears in his eyes)*
My name is Victor…

VICTOR (O.S.)

…Frankenstein.

Dissolve into: establishing shot of Frankenstein mansion on a sunny day.

CAPTION:
Geneva 1773

VICTOR (V.O)

"Hear my story, Captain Walton, and be warned…"

We hear a harpsichord begin playing a waltz as—

～

GRAND BALLROOM, FRANKENSTEIN MANSION
Day

—a wider angle reveals a huge, magnificent blue ballroom.

Victor (age 7) is waltzing with his Mother, a warm and beautiful woman, whom he clearly adores. Mrs. Moritz is seated at the harpsichord. Beside her sits her daughter Justine, age 4, her eyes fixed on Victor. Victor's Mother laughs to the rhythm of the waltz:

VICTOR

Mother, Mother!

MOTHER

My wonderful son, Victor. You are the handsomest, brightest, cleverest, most wonderfulest boy in the whole world.

She hugs him and they fall over onto the floor.

MRS. MORITZ

Madam, you will spoil the boy, really.

An enormous door swings open. Mrs. Moritz stops playing. Victor's Father enters, ushering in a somber and beautiful Elizabeth, age 6. Though dressed in somewhat shabby mourning clothes, she carries herself like a gypsy princess. Passion and pride shine in her eyes. Mrs. Moritz rises immediately, Mother and Victor kneel up.

FATHER

Leave us now, Mrs. Moritz.

MRS. MORITZ *(smiling)*

Doctor.

MOTHER

Yes, Mrs. Moritz, and take your daughter with you.

MRS. MORITZ
(snaps at Justine)

Come along, Justine.

Mrs. Moritz takes Justine's hand. Justine gazes back at Victor and Elizabeth as her mother whisks her off.

MOTHER

Victor. This is Elizabeth. She's coming to live with us.

FATHER

She has lost both her mother and father to the scarlet fever, Victor. She's an orphan now.

MOTHER

You must think of her as your own sister. You must look after her. And be kind to her. Always.

Victor walks slowly towards Elizabeth and Father pushes her forward. They meet in the middle of the room. Elizabeth proffers her hand and they shake on it.

FRANKENSTEIN MANSION, VICTOR'S ATTIC WORKSHOP
A night about ten years later

Closeup on a candle. Pull back to reveal a teenaged Victor sitting at a worktable with the beginnings of a mechanical dog strewn around. He has been making notes; pen and ink are in front of him, books piled everywhere.

Victor is in a meditative mood, staring into the flame of the candle, slowly passing his index finger back and forth through the flame, like a small child amazed to discover that he can play with fire without getting burned.

Victor's Mother enters softly. She watches Victor from the shadows for a moment, as if seeing him as a youngster once more. Unconsciously she touches her belly—and we see that she is heavily pregnant. Victor looks up and sees her.

VICTOR

How is the immiment arrival?

MOTHER

A little frisky today.
(pause)

When you were a little boy, you used to chase fire-flies in the fields.

VICTOR

Yes, and when I tried to trap them in my jars, they died.

MOTHER

Yes, do you remember how you cried?

VICTOR (*laughing*)

Yes.

MOTHER

Because you wanted them to keep glowing at your bedside to light you as you read. You were so hungry for knowledge. Such a serious little boy.
(*pause*)
And such an earnest young man you've become. All these strange and ancient books!

(*she picks up a book and examines it*)
You'll become an even greater doctor than your father. Life should not be all study, Victor. There's such fun to be had.

With a smile on her face, she steals the piece of paper Victor has been writing on.

VICTOR (*laughing*)

Give me that back!

She runs away, laughing back at him.

MOTHER

No.

VICTOR

Give me that back, Mother!

He chases her out of the room, both laughing and joking.

MANSION BALLROOM
Same Day

The Frankenstein family sweep before our eyes, waltzing away from camera to reveal Victor, intense and handsome as he approaches manhood. Elizabeth is a blossoming and graceful beauty. Victor dances with Mother and Elizabeth with Father.

Mrs. Moritz is still conducting the lessons, but the person at the harpsichord is now an older Justine. Victor's Mother is showing her pregnancy with a radiant bloom. Everyone is enjoying themselves immensely. The scene is celebratory, joyful, happy.

MRS. MORITZ
…And twirl….

The dancers work their way across the vast room.

MRS. MORITZ *(continued)*
Gallop…change partners!

The four of them start swapping partners as they sweep across the room. They continue to dance within inches of camera, until finally their bodies wipe frame—

MRS. MORITZ *(continued)*
Down this side…run along…that's it…excellent!

They all dance energetically around the room, but Mother has to stop and is scolded playfully by Father.

FATHER
You mustn't exert yourself, Caroline.

MOTHER
I know.

FATHER
Caroline, please.

Mother smiles at her husband as he leads her to the piano. Victor and Elizabeth dance on, watched by the mothers.

MRS. MORITZ
(to Victor and Elizabeth)
You'll be the envy of all the young ladies and gentlemen!

They're certainly the envy of Justine, who gazes at Victor as he sweeps Elizabeth into his arms with a flourish. She isn't concentrating and fumbles on the keyboard. Her mother throws her a look of reproval:

MRS. MORITZ
Justine!

Flustered, she puts her attention back on the keyboard. Victor notices Justine's discomfiture.

VICTOR
Please, Justine, may I have this dance?

Justine blushes and stands and they are about to dance when Mother suddenly faints to the floor. They rush in.

VICTOR
Mother…!

FATHER
Mrs. Moritz!

MANSION BEDROOM
Night

Victor's Mother in labor, lying in a birthing chair. The labor is not going well. Pain, sweat, screams. An exchange of looks between Mrs. Moritz, Father, and Justine.

Mrs. Moritz and Justine desperately tend to Mother, clenching her hands as she writhes with pain. Father kneels between her legs, mopping the blood as he tries desperately to save the baby.

MRS. MORITZ *(to Mother)*
That's it…
(urgently to Father)
Sir. *(beat)* You must make a decision.

FATHER *(paralyzed, anxious)*
How can I? The baby is in the wrong position. I can't proceed…unless…

MOTHER *(fighting the pain)*
Cut me. Save the baby.

Mrs. Moritz passes Father a scalpel. He lifts Mother's nightgown and inserts the knife. We pan off to black.

MANSION, DOWNSTAIRS PARLOR
Night

A storm is raging, rain drumming the window glass. We hear screaming in the house. Victor look-

ing out of a window. Elizabeth is with him. They turn to sit at the window seat. She squeezes his arm, trying to reassure him.

ELIZABETH
She'll be all right. Father's the finest doctor in Geneva.

Outside, on the grounds of the estate, a massive bolt of lightning hammers from the sky, hitting the oak tree that had stood for centuries on the lawn in front of the mansion. The tree top falls and the stump burns to a smoldering ruin.

Back to the parlor: On Victor and Elizabeth as they stand up to look at the ruins of the tree.

Cut to:

FATHER
I've killed my wife.

The Grand Ballroom. Victor and Elizabeth turn to see Father coming down the stairs.

VICTOR
Father…

Victor and Elizabeth tear across the ballroom and race up the great staircase. Father coming down in a daze, blood on his hands. Victor drives past him. Elizabeth pauses.

FATHER *(numb)*
I did everything I could.

Elizabeth follows Victor on up the stairs. Father sinks onto the stairs, staring at the blood on his hands.

FATHER
(repeats over and over)
I did everything I could…

Shift to Bedroom. Victor runs in to see his Mother hanging limply in the birthing chair, a lifeless heap. Justine, looking distraught, is trying to tidy the room.

VICTOR *(weeping gently)*
Bring her back. Please bring her back.

Elizabeth enters and stands in the doorway in shock.

    Somewhere O.S. we hear a baby begin to cry. We follow the camera as it pans over to Mrs. Moritz, who is cradling Victor's newborn baby brother. William.

Dissolve to:

WOODLAND LAKE, FRANKENSTEIN ESTATE
Day

Wide shot of sky and trees and sunlight. A welcome calm after the horror of Mother's death.

    Victor, in funereal black, stands alone at the water's edge. Still, reflective, somber. The passing of his Mother is the first real loss he has ever experienced. He looks to the heavens as if seeking an answer, then turns to walk away and we

Dissolve to:

MANSION, VICTOR'S ATTIC WORKSPACE
Day

Closeup on Victor's hands as he tears pages, one by one, out of his books. His manner is methodical with suppressed emotion, numb.

    Justine, sitting opposite him, reaches across and puts her hand on his, trying to stop him.

JUSTINE
Victor, stop it! Stop!

VICTOR
I want her back, Justine.

JUSTINE
I do too. But it isn't possible. Victor, you can't abandon this now. There is so much you could achieve. You have a calling to fight sickness and disease, you—

VICTOR *(interrupting)*
But that isn't enough, Justine. We have to fight…
(It hits him like a thunderbolt.)
…death itself.

Justine sees the passion in his eyes. She's horrified.

JUSTINE
You can't interfere with nature, Victor.

VICTOR *(rapid, intense)*
We "interfere" with nature every time we light a fire. We interfere with nature every time we use the skin of beasts to protect us from the elements.

JUSTINE
No, that isn't the same…

VICTOR
It is in our nature to interfere. It is in our nature to strive for a better world.

45

> I need not describe the feelings of those whose dearest ties are rent by that most irreparable evil, the void that presents itself to the soul, and the despair that is exhibited on the countenance. It is so long before the mind can persuade itself that she, whom we saw every day, and whose very existence appeared a part of our own, can have departed for ever—that the brightness of a beloved eye can have been extinguished, and the sound of a voice so familiar, and dear to the ear, can be hushed, never more to be heard.

We're tight on his eyes—the same intensity his Mother feared.

VICTOR
We're on the brink of a scientific revolution.
(picks up a book)
And we have the ancients, the mystics and the alchemists. Between them, there is an answer. And I will not stop until I find it.

Dissolve to:

FRANKENSTEIN MANSION
Day

LEGEND:
Three years later.

Inside the mansion: We see a candle arrangement which drives a wheel, which in turn drives the strings of a puppet dog.

ELIZABETH (O.S.)
But Victor, you've been here for hours.

She comes into shot, looking at the dog.

VICTOR
Yes, creating the world's first mechanical dog. Don't you think Mother would have been pleased?

ELIZABETH (at the dog)
Um…woof…woof!
(to Victor)
Please come outside, Victor. It's such a beautiful day!

Victor is at the other end of his work bench, adjusting a metal rod.

VICTOR
Go away. I'm busy.

Elizabeth moves over and picks up a long metal instrument.

ELIZABETH
What's this?

Victor now reaches down into a vat and pulls out a wriggling eel.

VICTOR
It's for spraying down the electric eels.

Elizabeth tries it and sprays Victor in the face. She laughs hysterically. Victor abandons his eels and begins to chase her around the room as she continues to spray the water at him.

VICTOR
Put it down, it's not for playing with. Put it down!

They continue to chase about the room, laughing hysterically, and we move off them up through the rafters to the cupola.

Dissolve to:

ALPINE RIDGE
Day

A cliff face: We move up it to see Victor, Elizabeth, Justine, and Willie at the top. They turn and run along the ridge, Elizabeth trying to fly a kite, Justine and Willie getting left behind.

When I was about fifteen years old, we had retired to our house near Belrive, when we witnessed a most violent and terrible thunderstorm. It advanced from behind the mountains of Jura; and the thunder burst at once with frightful loudness from various quarters of the heavens. I remained, while the storm lasted, watching its progress with curiosity and delight. As I stood at the door, on a sudden I beheld a stream of fire issue from an old and beautiful oak, which stood about twenty yards from our house; and so soon as the dazzling light vanished, the oak had disappeared, and nothing remained but a blasted stump. When we visited it the next morning, we found the tree shattered in a singular manner. It was not splintered by the shock, but entirely reduced to thin ribbands of wood. I never beheld any thing so utterly destroyed.

ELIZABETH
Willie!

VICTOR
Come on!

ELIZABETH
Yes, come on! After all, we should be grateful to Victor for abandoning his experiments for one afternoon.

VICTOR
Who says I have?

ELIZABETH
What do you mean?

VICTOR
Ah! Look.

He turns and points to the distance. A black storm cloud, bristling with lightning, is heading straight for them. The smiles on the girls' faces vanish.

JUSTINE
We're all going to die.

ELIZABETH
You knew this was going to happen!

VICTOR (*brightly*)
Not for certain, but I had hoped the conditions would be right. They're quite common up here at this time of the year. I've never seen one quite as large as that, though. Look, isn't it wonderful?

ELIZABETH
We must take cover. A tree!

VICTOR
No! That's just the wrong thing to do. It's potentially a much larger conductor than we are.

JUSTINE (*desperate*)
Victor, what about Willie?

ELIZABETH
What are we to do?

VICTOR
Come on.

He leads them off. The cloud gets nearer and nearer.

We go into quick cuts—montage: Victor opens the picnic basket and reveals, along with the picnic, lightning conductor equipment. Elizabeth opens a shooting stick and pushes it into the ground. Victor takes out a folded metal rod, extends it and fits on the lightning conductor, spreading out the fingers.

ELIZABETH
What is that?

Victor slots the metal rod through the handle of the shooting stick and also into the ground.

Justine and Willie are laying out the blankets on the grass in a star shape around the picnic basket and conductor.

Victor looks up and sees the cloud is almost on them.

VICTOR
Come on.

JUSTINE
Willie!

VICTOR
Get down quickly, everybody lie down quickly…come on, Justine.

From high above we see them take their positions on the rugs, lying on their stomachs. Elizabeth is the last one down and reaches out for Willie, who is hiding his head in his arms. Justine has a hand on his head and the other holding Victor's hand. Victor looks up and then takes cover as the cloud approaches. They wait.

ELIZABETH

Victor?

VICTOR

It will be fine. Stay where you are.

Aerial shot: the four of them lying on the rug.

ELIZABETH

Victor, I hope you know what you are doing.

Willie moves to get up.

JUSTINE

Willie *(pulling him down)*.

ELIZABETH *(impatiently)*

Victor…

VICTOR

Wait. *(beat)* One, two, three…

From a distance we see the cloud right above them; the lightning strikes the conductor, which rattles madly.

VICTOR

Now!

Victor smiles and gets to his knees. Elizabeth does the same. She looks at her hands in wonder. Tiny, livid snakes of electricity dancing all over her hands. She puts her fingers together; a spark leaps across. She looks at Victor and they both hold out their fingers—another spark leaps across.

They put their faces close together, and a spark leaps between their noses. They laugh with delight. Justine and Willie also look in wonder at the sparks on themselves.

VICTOR

How do you feel, Elizabeth?

ELIZABETH

Alive.

Cut to:

MANSION, GRAND BALLROOM
Night

Three years later.

Victor is in the prime of manhood. Elizabeth, womanly now, radiates poise and intelligence. Justine has also grown into an attractive woman, although somewhat nervous and intense. She dances with William (age 7), looking charmingly formal.

The dance ends with a great flourish, Elizabeth being lifted into the air by Victor. The guests applaud. Victor and Elizabeth kiss.

CLAUDE *(on stairs)*
Ladies and gentlemen…!

The dancers stop. The orchestra falls silent. Justine hides her disappointment as they gather round.

FATHER *(unsteady, shy)*
Dear friends, as you probably know, tomorrow my dear son Victor leaves me to pursue what I'm sure will be an illustrious career in a profession with which I myself am not altogether unassociated.
(warm laughter)
My one regret is that his mother…my late wife…is not here to share the pride which…our son fills me with tonight…

Claude passes Father a leather-bound journal.
     On Father: close to tears as he takes the book from Claude. Victor is also close to tears.

FATHER *(continued)*
Yes…she wanted you to have this, Victor, on your graduation.

He opens the cover of the book.

FATHER *(continued)*
In it she has written, "This is the journal of Victor Frankenstein." The rest of its leaves are blank, waiting to be filled with the deeds of a noble life.

OUTSIDE THE MANSION
Night

Victor and Elizabeth dancing outside the ballroom. Guests can be glimpsed behind them, dancing in the ballroom. The orchestra can be heard, faintly. Their faces are close together and they nearly kiss— Elizabeth breaks off, flustered.

ELIZABETH
We'd better go in before they miss us.

VICTOR
Just a little while longer, please.

He starts to walk past the long windows and she follows.

VICTOR *(continued)*
I don't know when we'll be alone together again.

He seems agitated.

ELIZABETH *(laughing gently)*
Oh dear, Victor.

VICTOR *(also laughing)*
I shall miss you laughing at me.

ELIZABETH
I'll miss you making me laugh.

He stops and turns to her.

VICTOR
So…how do brothers and sisters say goodbye?

ELIZABETH *(slowly)*
Perhaps they never have to.

VICTOR *(remembering)*
I won't if you won't.

Their eyes searching each other…and then… he kisses her: a long, hungry, hot, wet kiss. She leans into him, returning his passion.

VICTOR *(anguished)*
I can't leave you.

ELIZABETH
I don't want you to go.

VICTOR
I love you so much.

ELIZABETH
I love you too.

They kiss again, hungry, intense.

VICTOR
Are you my sister?

ELIZABETH *(smiling with certainty)*
Sister, friend, lover…

Victor gets to his knees.

VICTOR
…wife?

She looks at him. There can be no other man.

ELIZABETH
Yes.

VICTOR *(impetuous, hot)*
Then come with me to Ingolstadt. Marry me now.

ELIZABETH *(reeling)*
No.

VICTOR *(standing)*
Then I'll stay here.

She kisses him.

ELIZABETH
I want more than anything else in the world to be your wife…but as long as you are away, I belong here. I want to make this house live again. I want to make this a great home for our children. And now you must go and do the great things you need to do.

VICTOR *(tender)*
I want you so much.

He presses into her again, savoring the moment, not wanting it to end.

ELIZABETH *(clear, true)*
I will be here when you return…each holiday, every visit…and then on our wedding night…

Another kiss. Lustful and steamy.

VICTOR *(assenting)*
Until our wedding night.

An extended moment. Elizabeth holds out her hand and Victor reaches to take it. Closeup on their clasped hands, a mirror image of when they shook hands as children to seal their bond.

ALPINE ROAD
Day

High on a ridge overlooking the Alps stands a monument. Victor rides up to it and dismounts. He stands in front of it and places a sprig of flowers below the legend which reads "Beloved Wife and Mother…Caroline Beaufort Frankenstein." He straightens and looks at the statue.

VICTOR
Oh, Mother, you should never have died. No one need ever die. I will stop this, I will stop this. I promise.

Cut to:

INGOLSTADT
Day

Close on big wooden gates opening. Townfolk rush in.
Victor steers the horse through the gates of the city as they open early in the morning and into the main square, seething with city life, the market already busy as it is being set up.

FRAU BRACH'S BOARDING HOUSE
Day

Frau Brach trudges heavily up a long, steep, narrow flight of outside stairs followed by her lovable dog, Putzi. Victor follows along behind.

FRAU BRACH
There are a lot of stairs, I'm afraid. How was your journey?

VICTOR
Very good, thank you.

Inside the boarding house, in a garret: They move into a narrow corridor and then on into a bedroom, Frau Brach chattering all the way.

FRAU BRACH
Good, I'm pleased. Well, as I said, we've only got attic space.

VICTOR
But that's absolutely fine. But there are no other keys, and just this one entrance? Good. And, as I mentioned, there will be no requirements for other help. I shall be quite self-sufficient, thank you.

He bends to pat the dog.

VICTOR
Hello, girl.

FRAU BRACH
Putzi likes you.

Victor moves off into an immensely long room: massive vaulted beams and grimy dormer windows that dimly filter in the light. At one end of the room there is a dusty upright piano. He turns towards her.

VICTOR
This will be perfect.

UNIVERSITY GATES

Day

A monumental stone structure. Cast into its arches the legend "Knowledge is power only through God."

KREMPE (O.S.)

...The foolish and vain force their views by the rod, but knowledge is power only through God—a motto easily forgotten by you young men in a hurry.

Inside the lecture hall, Professor Krempe, a squat little man, paces before the packed galleries of eager young students who are laughing and applauding.

KREMPE

...but perhaps the greatest mistake that all students make during their time here is to suppose they can ever have an original or creative thought. We have all imagined *that* in our time.

He looks over to another professor, Waldman, by the door.

KREMPE

But, gentlemen, you have not come here in order to think for yourselves. You are here to learn how to think for your patients. You must learn, therefore, in the first place, to submit yourselves to the established laws of physical reality.

VICTOR

But surely, Professor, you don't intend we disregard more...philosophical approaches.

Everyone in the lecture hall turns to look at Victor.

KREMPE

Philosophical?

VICTOR

Those which stir the imagination as well as the intellect. As in Paracelsus, for example.

This reference is lost on all but Waldman.
    On Waldman: looking at Victor and taking an interest in him.

KREMPE
Paracelsus. An arrogant and foolish Swiss.

VICTOR
Albertus Magnus.

Up among the students, Henry Clerval leans out and shoots an amused look in Victor's direction.

KREMPE (moving back to the rail)
His nonsense was exploded 500 years ago!

VICTOR
Cornelius Agrippa.

KREMPE
What is your name?

VICTOR
Victor Frankenstein, sir. Of Geneva.

The entire class laughs.

KREMPE
Ah, another Swiss. (more laughter from the class)
Well, Frankenstein, here at the University of Ingolstadt we teach, and indeed attempt to advance, the study of medicine, chemistry, biology, physics. We study hard science…

VICTOR
But surely, Professor, the greatest possible advances lie in combining…

KREMPE (sharply interrupting)
…we *do not* study the ravings of lunatics and alchemists hundreds of years in their graves. Because their kind of amateur, fanatical, fantastical speculation does not heal bodies or save lives! Only science can do that.
(Waldman leaves the lecture hall)
Now, have we your permission to continue?

Victor is flushed and humiliated. He'd like to say more, but wisely swallows his anger and leaves.

UNIVERSITY GATES
Day

A few townsfolk hang around, sullen, resentful. They view with contempt the "young gentlemen" emerging from the University gates. Victor, eyes ablaze, exits wearing a distinctive grey greatcoat. Henry catches up with Victor.

HENRY
Nice coat.

VICTOR (grimly)
Thank you.

HENRY
Don't take it too hard. It's just that Krempe doesn't approve of public humiliation.

VICTOR *(stopping)*
I am not mad.

HENRY
My dear fellow, of course you're not. In fact that's just the sort of thing I'd expect a perfectly rational person to say to a complete stranger.

Victor begins to smile at Henry's sarcasm.

HENRY *(continued)*
Henry Clerval, by the way, and I'm completely crazy.

VICTOR *(laughing)*
Victor Frankenstein.

HENRY
Of Geneva…

VICTOR
Yes, of Geneva.

HENRY
I noticed…

At that moment Schiller crashes into them.

SCHILLER
Why don't you look where I'm going.

He moves on through them and away.

HENRY *(moving on)*
That's Schiller, ornament of the playing field.

VICTOR
Really.

HENRY *(continued)*
He's new as well. You can tell because he goes around looking at things with his mouth open. *(a beat)* What are you here for?

VICTOR
Research.

HENRY *(heavily ironic)*
Very grand. I'm here to become a mere doctor. I'm told that has something to do with healing the sick.

58

Which is a pity, really, because I find sick people rather revolting.

As Henry gabbles on, Victor stops as he sees the shadowy figure of Waldman moving away to his coach.

HENRY *(continued)*
Still, I'll have a good time, get my degree—*if* I can stop failing anatomy—and settle down to relieve rich old ladies of their imaginary ailments, and *then* relieve their very real and beautiful daughters.

The coach drives off and they move on.

VICTOR
Who was that? He was at the lecture.

HENRY
Ah. That's Waldman.

VICTOR *(impressed)*
So that's Waldman.

HENRY
Interesting case. They say in his youth he could break into heaven and lecture God on science. Ran into trouble with the authorities a few years back. Something to do with illegal experiments.

VICTOR *(intrigued)*
What kind of experiments, I wonder?

(recovering)
So. What was it you were saying? Rich old ladies and their daughters?

HENRY
It's a life of sacrifice, I know, but someone's got to do it.

They stop, smiling at each other as Waldman's coach passes them, driving out of the city. Victor watches it go.

UNIVERSITY AUTOPSY ROOM
Day

An undissected corpse lies on the slab, partly covered in a sheet. A line is drawn across his forehead. Waldman, in smock, addresses a group of students that includes Victor, Henry, and Schiller. Waldman is delivering his remarks standing over the body.

WALDMAN
…and that is *why* the central nervous system and its crowning achievement, the brain, are as complicated and mysterious a set of organs as you are ever likely to encounter. Mr. Frankenstein, the incision is yours.

He hands over a scalpel to Victor. The other students watch as Victor deftly cuts a circle round the corpse's hairline. Waldman is impressed.

WALDMAN *(continued)*
Excellent. Mr. Clerval, you may remove the cranial lid.

On Henry: eyes widening before he quietly slips from frame in a swoon.

MANSION, GRAND BALLROOM, FIRESIDE
Night

We find Father coming down the stairs, carrying Willie on his shoulders, with Elizabeth as she reads Victor's letter aloud: the rest of the household gathering round them at the fireplace.

ELIZABETH
"Henry has now fully recovered and continues his struggle to pass anatomy...."

FATHER
I was always terrible at anatomy.

ELIZABETH
"...Professor Waldman is very tolerant of him and of myself. I am learning a great deal. Professor Waldman is remarkable..."

JUSTINE
So is Victor.

ELIZABETH
"…God bless you, all my love, Victor…"

MRS. MORITZ
That's very nice.

ELIZABETH
"…P.S. I've fallen in love…"

CLAUDE
I beg your pardon?

ELIZABETH
"…She's dark, sleek and beautiful, and always wags her tail whenever she sees me. Her name is Putzi and she's the friendliest sheepdog I've ever known.
(to herself)
P.P.S. Elizabeth—I dream of how your hair shines in the moonlight, of how your lips taste. I dream of your arms, and of your breasts…and of the time, on our wedding night…"

WILLIAM
(taking the letter from her)
What else does it say?

Elizabeth snatches the letter away from him.

ELIZABETH *(quickly, embarrassed)*
It says, I am working very hard and making lots of new friends. More coffee, anyone?

UNIVERSITY LECTURE HALL
Day

Krempe, mid-lecture, in the crowded hall. During the scene the camera circles the two men. There is a half-dissected body on the table.
    Krempe pulls off his wig in fury and slams it down on the body.

KREMPE *(furious)*
…Once and for all, Frankenstein, life is life, death is death. These things are real, they are absolute…

VICTOR
Now that is rubbish! And you know it. That premise has been repeatedly challenged by members of your own staff.

WALDMAN
This is outrageous.

In M. Waldman I found a true friend. His gentleness was never tinged by dogmatism; and his instructions were given with an air of frankness and good nature, that banished every idea of pedantry. I t was, perhaps, the amiable character of this man that inclined me more to that branch of natural philosophy which he professed, than an intrinsic love for the science itself. But this state of mind had place only in the first steps towards knowledge: the more fully I entered into the science, the more exclusively I pursued it for its own sake. That application, which at first had been a matter of duty and resolution, now became so ardent and eager, that the stars often disappeared in the light of morning whilst I was yet engaged in my laboratory.

VICTOR *(continued)*
Yes, you sir *(as he points to Waldman)*.

The shadowy figure of Waldman quickly leaves the hall.

WALDMAN *(as he leaves)*
I am not listening to this.

VICTOR
We don't know where life ends or death begins. Hair continues to grow after what we choose to call death. So do fingernails…

KREMPE
These are trivial examples, which can be easily explained.

VICTOR *(overlapping)*
We know that a man's brain may die but his heart and lungs may continue to pump and breathe.
(screams at Krempe)
Now, you know that!

KREMPE *(exploding)*
Mr. Frankenstein of Geneva, I warn you that what you are suggesting is not only illegal, it is immoral!

VICTOR
Rubbish!

He stalks out of the room.

BACK STREET NEAR UNIVERSITY GATES
Evening

Victor and Henry striding away. Victor writes in his thick, well-worn leather journal.

HENRY
(peering over Victor's shoulder, mocking)
Dear diary, why does no one understand me? P.S. I am not mad…

Victor is grabbed by Waldman and thrown back onto a wall.

WALDMAN
You. Explain yourself.

VICTOR *(suddenly thrown)*
Professor, I'm sorry. Listen. I came here, Professor, to learn all about the new science. Galvanism, Franklin's experiments. The combination of modern disciplines with ancient knowledge in an attempt to protect and to create…

WALDMAN *(intense)*
To create what…?

VICTOR
Sir, we can change things. We can make things better. You know that. We're on the verge of undreamt-of discoveries. If only we had the courage to ask the right questions. Now you must help me, please.

WALDMAN
Come on.

HENRY
(trying to stop him from following Waldman)
Victor.

VICTOR
Come on, Henry.

WALDMAN'S HOME WORKSHOP
Night

An artist's nook. The door opens and Waldman comes in, Victor and Henry close behind, gazing around.

Victor leads Henry through a partially hidden door into a cramped but fascinating mini-laboratory. Victor is fascinated and delighted by what he sees.

WALDMAN *(to Henry)*
Lock the door.

Henry turns and locks the door. Waldman turns to Victor.

WALDMAN
Now, for thousands of years the Chinese have based their medical science on the belief that the human body is a chemical engine run by energy streams.

Henry is glancing in a old book lying on the table in front of him.

WALDMAN *(turning)*
Don't touch that!

Henry quickly closes the book and moves away.

WALDMAN
Their doctors treat patients by inserting needles like this…*(hands over a needle)*…into the flesh at various key points to manipulate these electric streams.

He directs Victor's attention to an ancient Chinese silk on the wall. It depicts the human body from front and side angles. Acupuncture points are clearly marked.

VICTOR
I see.

WALDMAN
Now, look at this.

Waldman moves and pulls off a green cloth to reveal the arm of a chimpanzee pricked by acupuncture needles, from which copper mounting pins trail wires to a small panel of switches. The switches, in turn, are connected to a series of galvanic batteries.

Waldman clips the connectors up. Henry and Victor let out a shriek, jumping backwards as the arm twitches.

WALDMAN *(to Henry)*
Go on, touch it.

Henry places a nervous finger on the back of the hand.

HENRY
It feels warm.

Henry continues to touch the hand as Waldman tries another connector. A sudden spark in the equipment, and the hand grabs Henry's.

HENRY *(continued)*
Yes, well, how do you do.

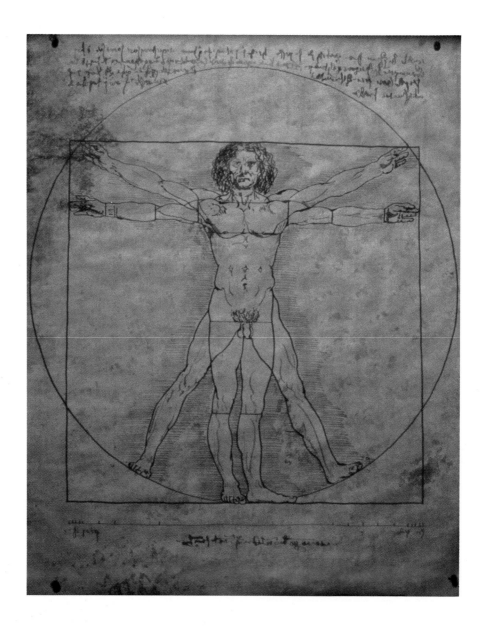

But the hand won't let go. It is increasing its grip on Henry, pulling him down onto his knees. The mood changes.

HENRY (*in genuine panic*)
Turn it off!

WALDMAN (*troubled*)
I can't. It's not working.

Tension and fear. Henry is in trouble. Victor attacks the situation with a sort of controlled frenzy.

VICTOR (*calm, clear*)
Try to stay calm, Henry. It's simply a matter of reducing the polarity between your body and the arm. A monkey's arm is basically the same as a human's…

HENRY (*through clenched teeth*)
No arm is this strong!

WALDMAN
The circuit is in reverse.

VICTOR
Then this must work…

Victor clips on a last connector. A spark. The hand releases Henry. Waldman casts Victor an admiring glance.

VICTOR
Let me help you, Professor.

A beat. Waldman eyes him.

WALDMAN
You shall, of course, tell no one.

HENRY *(under his breath)*
They wouldn't believe you anyway.

On the chimpanzee's arm: now gently pulsating of its own accord. Henry looks astounded.

FRANKENSTEIN MANSION, GARDEN
Day

Elizabeth, wearing a red velvet cloak, is sitting on some garden steps, writing on her knees. It's a letter to Victor.

ELIZABETH
"Mrs. Moritz continues to love and torment Justine in equal measure. Willie grows more precocious every day, and Father almost expires with pride at the very thought of you and your work…And I… well, I miss you very much…Please write soon, Victor."

Cut into:

WALDMAN'S PARLOR
Night

That night, over dinner and wine in Waldman's parlor: Victor and Henry are almost in their cups. Waldman maintains a watchful silence.

VICTOR
…I'm serious. Take vaccine, for instance. Thirty years ago the entire concept of vaccine was unheard of. Now we save lives everyday, but *that* isn't the whole answer.

HENRY
What do you mean?

VICTOR
That sooner or later the best way to cheat death will be to create life.

HENRY *(through a mouthful of food)*
Oh, now you have gone too far. There's only one God, Victor.

VICTOR
Leave God out of this. Listen, if you love someone and they have a sick heart, wouldn't you give them a healthy one?

HENRY *(stunned)*
Impossible…

VICTOR
No. It's not impossible. We can do it. We're steps away from it…And if we can replace one part of a man, we can replace every part. And if we can do that, we can…design a life, a being that will not grow old or sicken, one that will be stronger than us, better than us, one that will be more intelligent than us, more civilized than us…

HENRY *(aghast)*
In our lifetime?

Victor is about to answer when, with unguarded vehemence:

WALDMAN
No!

An embarrassed pause.

VICTOR
How close did you get, Professor?

WALDMAN
Too close.

Waldman shudders at the memory. Shame and self-disgust cloud his face. There is a look between them. Victor rushes to the bookcase and pulls out the book that Henry had previously been drawn to.
    A look between the two men.

VICTOR *(urgent)*
Professor, I beg you, let me see these notes.

WALDMAN *(forceful)*
No. My work now, and its application, lies exclusively in the *preservation of life.* I abandoned my other researches many years ago.

VICTOR
Why?

WALDMAN
Because they resulted in abomination.

Cut to:

POORHOUSE
Day

Camera tracks through a city poorhouse. Ingolstadt is in crisis. Panicked people getting vaccinated against smallpox. The "doctors" in attendance are all Ingolstadt medical students performing community service.

We find Victor, Henry, and Schiller giving out vaccinations. They are all working urgently.

A Sharp-Featured Man is walking with the crowd, terrified about getting his vaccination. The man bristles with an unpredictable and ferocious nervous energy. He is blind in one eye, one-legged, and drunk. Though small, he has a torso of enviable strength. He is dragged up to Waldman's bench by two guards.

MAN *(snarling)*
Yer not stickin' that in me! Got a pox in it, I hear tell!

ROUGH WOMAN
Pox? They givin' us pox?

MAN
That's right, pox.

WALDMAN
(holding up an instrument)
No, it's not pox, it's a vaccine that will prevent a plague in this city.

ROUGH WOMAN
What's that?

WALDMAN
A tiny harmless amount of anti-smallpox serum.

MAN
You just said pox!

WALDMAN *(angry)*
I said it's harmless. It's a necessary precaution without which this godforsaken city would be put in immediate quarantine.

Victor and Henry pause at their work. Concerned, they drift closer. Murmurs of "Plague…pox" can be heard in the background. The Sharp-Featured Man is cornered.

MAN
You doctors kill people. I don' care what you say, you're not stickin' that in me!

WALDMAN
Yes I am. It's the law. Sit him down, somebody. Come on.

MAN *(struggling)*
You're not sticking that in me…

He is pushed down onto the bench as Waldman prepares to vaccinate. Unseen by Waldman, the Sharp-Featured Man suddenly pulls a knife from

66

the handhold on his crutch, stabs Waldman in the stomach and runs off.

Waldman sits back, hand pressed to his sternum, lips tight.

VICTOR

Sir?

HENRY

Professor?

VICTOR (more desperate)

Sir?!

WALDMAN (softly)

Oh, God.

Blood pumping through his fingers. He collapses. The poorhouse erupts into a frenzy. Victor, Henry, and Schiller run to Waldman's aid. As they reach

Waldman, Victor screams, "Find him!" pointing as if to the Sharp-Featured Man.

UNIVERSITY OPERATING THEATER
Day

Waldman is on the table, Victor and Henry desperately working to save his life. Schiller is helping. Masses of blood.

VICTOR

Come on. Come on…

HENRY

It's no use, Victor. He's gone.

VICTOR

No! No!

HENRY

Let him go.

VICTOR

No! No, Henry! It shouldn't happen, Henry. It shouldn't happen.
(*pushing over a table*)
It *needn't* happen.

TOWN SQUARE
Day

A grey day. Waldman's sharp-featured murderer stands ranting on the scaffold. A large crowd has gathered and is shouting abuse.

MAN

To hell with you…Whatever you say, whatever you call it, you doctors are killers…you murder people. Evil, you're evil…you're the ones who deserve to die. God will punish you…He will punish you.
(*as the hood goes on*) God will punish you!

The noose goes around his neck. He is pushed from the gallows by the town officials.

We hear the thump of the body dropping, the crack of a snapping neck. The crowd cheers.

WALDMAN'S HOME WORKSHOP
Night

View on the doors to Waldman's workshop. We see a crowbar force them open, and Victor comes in.

We see the anatomical drawing ripped from the door. The Chinese acupuncture chart rolled up. Waldman's notebook opened up.

Tracking shot: The door off its hinges. Some candles alight. We find Victor poring over Waldman's notes.

VICTOR (*breathless*)

My God, you were so close. Of course. The power. The materials were wrong…you needed auxiliary sources.

He picks up an anatomical drawing of a man, heavily annotated with symbols and mathematical formulae.

VICTOR (continued)
Yes…"Experiment…a failure. Resulting re-animant malformed and hideous to behold. This factor clearly dependent on appropriate raw materials." …raw materials

TOWN SQUARE
Night

That night: It is dark as Hades. A flash of lightning and a crash of thunder. The dead man still hangs from the scaffold, lashed by the wind.

Victor emerges from the shadows carrying a lit torch. He gazes intently at the dead man. A knife cuts through a rope. The body drops…

TAVERN
Night

Henry and Victor sitting in the corner of a tavern. A bottle is put down on the table.

VICTOR
Come on, Henry…

HENRY
I can't help you. Victor, I can't.

VICTOR
You mean you won't. What are you frightened of?

HENRY
Everything—what do you think? What if the authorities were to find out…?

VICTOR
Listen. We do this in secret. I've got the raw materials. I've got Waldman's journal. Together we know more than Krempe's whole staff.

HENRY
You stole Waldman's journal?

VICTOR
We owe it to him to complete this work. He was one step away.

HENRY
He never wanted this.

VICTOR
He couldn't face it. There's a difference.

HENRY
Even if it were possible, and even if you had the right, which you don't, to make this decision for us—can you imagine for one second that there wouldn't be a terrible price to pay?

VICTOR
I think for the chance to defeat death and disease, to let people on this earth have the chance of life, healthy sustained life for everyone, to allow people who love each other to be together forever…for that…Yes, I think it's a risk worth taking.

Cut to establishing shot outside Victor's garret.

VICTOR'S GARRET
Day

The dead murderer lies covered in a sheet on a slab. Victor moves from the window to the body, lifting the sheet to study the truncated leg. He moves on up the body to lift the sheet up to study the face closely.

Victor is working on the corpse of the murderer. He marks the truncated leg where it is to be taken off and then marks the diseased face and around the blind eye and around the left shoulder.

He takes the scissors and starts to cut the murderer's hair, then marks the place of inciscion.

We hear the sound of the saw O.S.

FRANKENSTEIN MANSION
Night

Establishing shot of mansion at night. Cut to Elizabeth at her desk lit by candlelight.

ELIZABETH
(reads aloud as she writes)
"And what of Henry and Professor Waldman, you hardly mention them now?…and what of you?… Please, Victor, write to us soon and tell us you are safe and well. And tell us what you're doing…please."

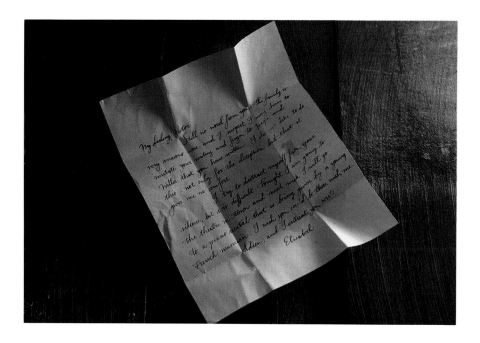

GRAVEYARD
Night

A graveyard: Victor is at the gates of a crypt, with a pry bar in his hands. He's nervous, working up his courage, as he opens the chains.

> VICTOR
> Raw materials. That's all they are. Tissue to be re-used.

He goes in. The lid of a coffin is eased off to reveal Waldman. Victor looks at him.

VICTOR'S GARRET
Night

Cut to: Victor packing the new brain in a trunk of ice.

MORTUARY
Night

A room full of the dead.

Victor is escorted in. He hands over money. We see, at the end of a row of bodies, the corpse of Schiller.

Victor moves to his body and lifts a cloth covering it to check one leg, as the camera pans up the corpse. Victor raises a glinting, razor-sharp meat cleaver as the pan ends on Schiller's face.

Cut to: establishing shot of exterior of Victor's garret. A flash of lightning.

VICTOR'S GARRET
Night

We find Victor working into the wee hours, hunched over his specimens, the candle flame flickering low. He refers back to Waldman's notes, makes notations in arcane books. He cuts the pages of Waldman's books and with great care pastes them into the journal.

> VICTOR *(reading)*
> Now, the assembled organs must have the designated nutrients and heat…and, crucially, more direct power.

He closes his journal, picking it up. Realizing…

Cut to: A butcher's block. Victor grabs a slab of fresh meat, dripping with blood. He slices it in half with a razor-sharp meat cleaver.

> VICTOR
> …more direct power.

He looks up at the waterproof sack and tosses the oozing carrion up into it. The sack judders and spasms as whatever is inside it throws itself on the fresh meat in a repulsive feeding frenzy. The noise is sickening.

FRANKENSTEIN ESTATE
Late Day

A magnificent backdrop of mountains against a cloudless blue sky. Elizabeth is marching along beside a lake, tearing up some letters. Justine follows, trying to catch up.

JUSTINE *(uncomprehending)*
But I don't understand. All these letters…you read them to us yourself. Every week.

ELIZABETH
I wrote them. I wrote the letters. He hasn't written to me in months.

JUSTINE *(shocked)*
Elizabeth!

ELIZABETH
Something horrific is happening to him. I can feel it. At first I wasn't sure, but I knew I had to hide it from Father. Now there are rumors of cholera…

JUSTINE *(firm, strong)*
I can take care of Father and Willie. You go to Ingolstadt.

ELIZABETH
No, that's not possible. He wouldn't want me there. He's probably found someone else.

Justine suddenly grabs her and turns Elizabeth to face her.

JUSTINE *(turning her around)*
If he were mine, I would have left already. But he isn't mine, he's yours. And you must go to him.

Elizabeth suddenly realizes Justine's feelings for Victor.

ELIZABETH
Oh, Justine, I didn't know how much Victor meant to you…

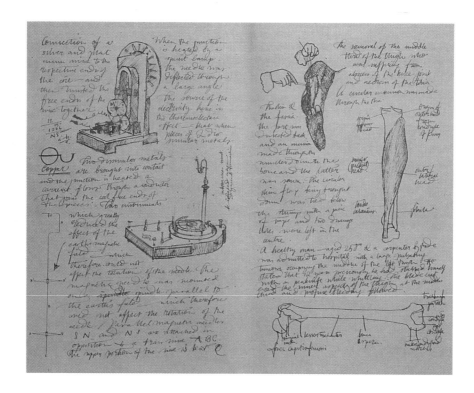

JUSTINE *(with great dignity)*
You don't have to say a word, Elizabeth. Just find him and bring him home.

Cut to:

CHARITY HOSPITAL MATERNITY WARD
Night

A woman in a birthing chair, screaming as she goes into labor. Her waters break, cascading into a steel bucket. One of the assistants snatches it up, scurries around the corner. Victor is waiting in the shadows. Money changes hands.

VICTOR'S GARRET
Night

Victor is examining the amniotic fluid. Boiling it off, working to synthesize it. He fills a metal scoop with the fluid and carries it over towards a dead but pulsing toad lying in a petri dish. He pours the fluid into a funnel, and pushes the liquid down a tube that goes into the toad.

VICTOR *(as he works)*
…amniotic fluid at optimum density and temperature…copper acupuncture needles piercing flesh at all key energy points…Now after removal of current, the dead toad should retain animation, but independently of external power sources.

He takes off the connector to the current, giving off a spark. To his delight, the toad continues to live of its own accord.

VICTOR
Yes, that's it…that's the combination…That's it!

On Victor: his triumph. He turns his back on the petri dish to make some notes in his journal as the camera moves in on the toad. Suddenly its back legs let out a strong kick, cracking the lid of the petri dish. Victor, ominously, does not notice this.

Scene shifts, another night: Victor pours the final drum of fluid into what appears to be a large copper vat. He dips his hand in, examines the consistency and smell. Angle widens, spinning slowly up to reveal that the vat is human in shape. A sarcophagus.

Victor stitches the arm onto the torso of Sharp-Featured Man with one of those big, awful curved needles, yanking up hard to draw the catgut tight. He is working fast, rushing the job.

Another view of the garret: The Creature lies on a pile of crates, draped like Christ in Michelangelo's *Pietá*. Beakers bubbling and dripping. Intravenous lines seeping and secreting. A chemical haze in the air.

Victor walks round the iron ring that hangs from the ceiling. He checks the multitude of bottles and lines holding various liquids that hang from it.

Victor collapses from exhaustion.

VICTOR'S GARRET
Day

His creation has finished taking the fluids. Grey daylight streams through the windows.

Victor is still lying where he collapsed the night before by the Creature's feet. There's a commotion in the street outside: shouting, horses' hooves clattering on cobblestone, an occasional scream or wail. Victor doesn't stir. Dead to the world.

Somebody starts pounding on the door. Victor rouses, takes a moment to remember where he is. He lurches up and pulls the sacking over his "patchwork man."

Outside, on the boarding house stairs, Henry is pounding. Behind him there is panic in the streets.

Victor races to the inner open door.

HENRY (O.S.)
Victor. Open the door.

VICTOR
What do you want?

No one can conceive the variety of feelings which bore me onwards, like a hurricane, in the first enthusiasm of success. Life and death appeared to me ideal bounds, which I should first break through, and pour a torrent of light into our dark world. A new species would bless me as its creator and source; many happy and excellent natures would owe their being to me. No father could claim the gratitude of his child so completely as I should deserve theirs. Pursuing these reflections, I thought, that if I could bestow animation upon lifeless matter, I might in process of time (although I now found it impossible) renew life where death had apparently devoted the body to corruption.

HENRY (O.S., *panicked*)
This cholera…it's an epidemic. The city's been placed under martial law. Are you listening to me, Victor?

VICTOR
Yes? And?

HENRY (O.S.)
The militia's arriving to quarantine the city. Most of us are getting out while we still can. Look, Krempe knows you're here, for God's sake! What if he tells the authorities?

VICTOR (*dismissively*)
Goodbye, Henry.

ELIZABETH (O.S.)
Victor, it's me. Elizabeth.

On Victor's shock: his anguish and conflict.

ELIZABETH (O.S.)
Can you hear me? Victor, I have to see you.

Victor braces himself for a self-inflicted wound.

VICTOR
Go away.

On Henry and Elizabeth on the other side of the door: their concern. Below them in the square, pandemonium reigns.

ELIZABETH
Please, Victor. I won't leave here until you see me.

VICTOR'S GARRET, HALLWAY AND BEDROOM
Day

Victor goes out into his hallway. He closes the inner doors and unbolts the main door.

VICTOR
Come in the side door.

Victor goes into the bedroom. Henry and Elizabeth enter.

VICTOR (O.S.)
Alone!

Elizabeth follows Victor into the bedroom. She is visibly appalled by the sight of him and the smell.

ELIZABETH (*walking forward*)
What has happened to you? How can you live here like this? And that stench.

She moves towards the laboratory door. Victor blocks her way, pushing her backwards.

VICTOR
Don't go in there.

ELIZABETH
We have to leave. This isn't safe.

VICTOR

No! I have to stay.

ELIZABETH

Even if it means you'll die?

VICTOR

Yes.

A beat. She is distraught.

ELIZABETH

Well, let me help you.

VICTOR

No, that's impossible.

ELIZABETH

We made a promise.

VICTOR (*sitting down*)

Don't.

ELIZABETH

Victor, I beg you…

VICTOR (*slowly, with difficulty*)

Look, I know this is difficult for you to understand, but I…cannot abandon this work now. It's too important, not just for me, but…believe me, for everyone, and it must…come first.

ELIZABETH

Before us?

VICTOR

Elizabeth, I love you so much but…

A beat.

ELIZABETH

Goodbye.

She leaves, going past Henry still at the door. He follows.

On Victor: his agony. He pushes open the door to the lab to look at his creation.

INGOLSTADT STREET
Day

A crowd in panic is rushing through the street. People are fleeing the city. Caught up amongst them are Elizabeth and Henry.

On Elizabeth: She pushes against the crowd. Suddenly they are separated and Henry can't see her.

HENRY

Elizabeth! Elizabeth!!

VICTOR'S GARRET
Night

Back in the garret: Victor is sitting as he scribbles in his journal:

VICTOR

"Time running out. Rioting in town. Decay of flesh accelerating. Must strike now…"

Victor gets up and marches through his workshop like Merlin the Magician. He switches on the Wimshurst machine and sets the steam engine wheels revolving as he passes.

He rounds the corner and we crane up to reveal for the first time Victor's Creation, lying on a metal grill, covered in a sheet.

Victor pulls off his robe, discarding it onto the floor, and moves over to the wall where he unties a rope. He pulls on the rope and the Creature on the grill begins to rise up towards the roof. Victor continues to pull and from below we see the body on the grill, arms out, not unlike the anatomical drawing.

The grill gets to the top. Victor moves over to another rope tied on the other side of his bedroom door. He unties it and then pulls hard on it and gives it a huge flick. This releases a wooden buffer hanging from the ceiling, which swings across to hit the grill and pushes it off onto the track running along the roof of the garret.

Victor runs after the body, and gets ahead, watching it as it goes, passing down the length of the lab. He climbs up to stand at the head end of the sarcophagus, looking down into the steaming liquid and then up to watch the body coming towards him.

Victor stands at the sarcophagus as he lowers the body on the grill down into the murky liquid. Once it is in position, he pulls off the shroud, which has covered it all this time.

Victor pulls the sarcophagus along its rail towards the fire as the lid comes down. He lines up the lid and the sarcophagus and slots them together. He tightens down the lid with the main lock on the lid. The bolts slide into place.

Victor guides a glass tube out of a huge bollock-shaped container hanging from the ceiling, its contents thrashing madly. The glass tube fits onto the lid of the sarcophagus and Victor fastens the two together.

Close on the acupuncture needles hanging on a wooden rack as Victor takes them off one by one,

fitting them through the holes in the sarcophagus and into the Creature's skin. One in its neck, one in its head, one in its knee.

The last needle is fitted into the foot and Victor moves off to the power terminals. He clips on the power connectors, and electricity races through the batteries and along the wires leading to the sarcophagus.

Victor races over to the glass tube of the sarcophagus and pulls a chain, which releases hundreds of eels down the tube and into the sarcophagus. The eels do whatever they do…

Victor, now standing on top of the sarcophagus, crawls forward on his stomach and looks through the porthole at the head end.

VICTOR
Live, live, live. *Live*…Yes!

Suddenly the Creature's eyes open.

Victor sits back in surprise. He leaps off the sarcophagus and races to the power supply, ripping off the clips. The power dies down, everything goes quiet and still.

The Creature goes limp inside the sarcophagus. Victor walks slowly over to his creation and looks in through the head porthole. Nothing is moving. Its eyes are closed.

VICTOR

No, no, no!

Slowly he turns and walks away, his experiment, all his work, a failure.

We move slowly in on the porthole by the Creature's hand. It taps on the glass. Inside the sarcophagus the Creature's eyes open—and register panic.

Victor, hearing the noise, turns. Is he imagining it?

The sarcophagus begins to convulse.

VICTOR

It's alive. It's alive...

He races towards the sarcophagus, which is now shaking madly, and reaches out to the main lock. But before he can get to the lead bolts, they snap from the power inside the sarcophagus.

Suddenly the lid flies off, sending Victor backwards into the spill tank as a wave of fluid lands on him.

The lid of the sarcophagus flies through the

I saw how the fine form of man was degraded and wasted; I beheld the corruption of death succeed to the blooming cheek of life; I saw how the worm inherited the wonders of the eye and brain. I paused, examining and analysing all the minutiae of causation, as exemplified in the change from life to death, and death to life, until from the midst of this darkness a sudden light broke in upon me—a light so brilliant and wondrous, yet so simple, that while I became dizzy with the immensity of the prospect which it illustrated, I was surprised that among so many men of genius, who had directed their inquiries towards the same science, that I alone should be reserved to discover so astonishing a secret.

Remember, I am not recording the vision of a madman. The sun does not more certainly shine in the heavens, than that which I now affirm is true. Some miracle might have produced it, yet the stages of the discovery were distinct and probable. After days and nights of incredible labour and fatigue, I succeeded in discovering the cause of generation and life; nay, more, I became myself capable of bestowing animation upon lifeless matter.

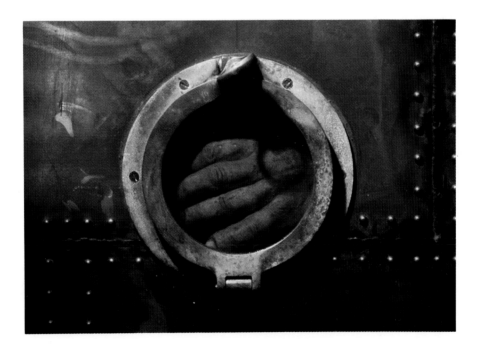

lab, sending shelves and equipment flying, finally ending up near the door, having knocked the shelf holding Victor's coat onto the ground.

Victor stares aghast at the sarcophagus. Slowly he gets to his feet and walks towards the now motionless vat. He walks up to the side of it, looking in, anticipating his creation is alive. But everything is still, no sign of life.

He looks down towards the feet—and suddenly the Creature flies up in front of him, grabbing for him. As he does this, the sarcophagus starts to topple off its rail and tips over onto its side, sending Victor and the Creature flying across the spill tank amongst the fluid and eels.

Slowly Victor looks up as the Creature crawls through the fluid.

VICTOR
I knew it could work. I knew it!

He moves over to his creation and tries to lift him to his feet. The Creature seems as helpless as the newly born.

VICTOR
Stand, please stand, come on…

The Creature, his vision hazy, manages to get to his feet.

VICTOR
(monologue during the following action)
Breathe, come on breathe.
Stand, you can stand, come on, come on, that's it.
What's wrong? What's wrong with you?
That's it, that's it.
You can do it, come on.
Stand, yes. Now walk. No, no.

With Victor still on his knees, they then slowly slide across the tank, the Creature managing to stand some of the time.

VICTOR
Let me help you, I'll help you to stand—the chains, the chains, over here.

Victor leads him over to some chains hanging from a bar and, in an attempt to help him to stand, he fits the Creature's arms into some ropes.

VICTOR
This must work, you're alive. What is wrong? What's wrong with you? Be careful of the rope— *look out!*

As Victor steps back, he loses his balance and, falling backwards, grabs a rope. A counterweight snaps, overloading the pulley, and the wooden bar

80

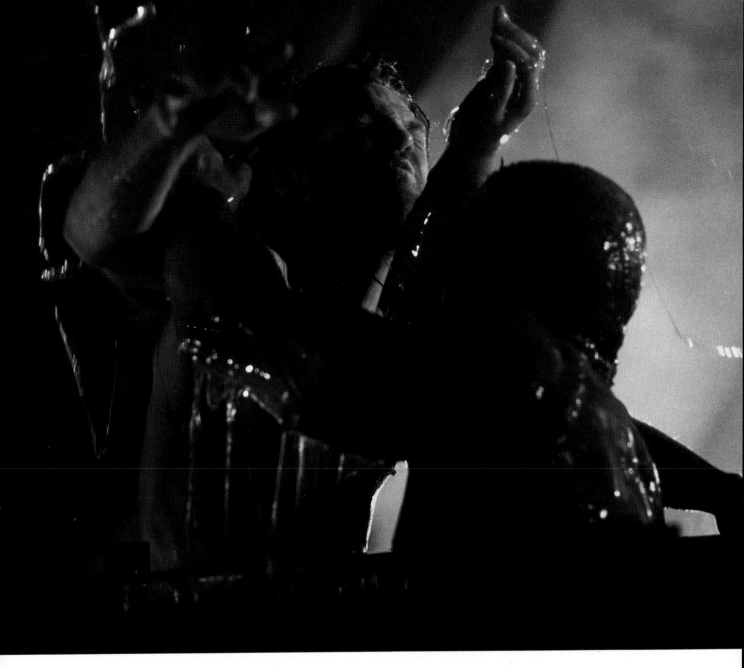

of chains begins to rise up, carrying the Creature with it, moaning and twitching.

A piece of wood comes down past him and hits him over the head. The bar of chains continues to rise and the Creature continues to struggle.

Victor stands, dripping fluid and goo, chest heaving, staring up at the Creature. The full horror sinks in.

Now the Creature's death throes are complete. Silence. Softly:

VICTOR
It's dead, it's dead, I've killed it! *(pause)*
What have I done? I gave it life and then I killed it.

Victor moves away, picks up his journal and walks away from the lifeless Creature hanging in the chains.

VICTOR *(writing in journal)*
"Massive birth defects. Greatly enhanced physical strength but the resulting re-animant is malfunctional and pitiful, and dead."

He closes the journal and places it in the pocket of his greatcoat.

VICTOR *(continued)*
"Tomorrow this journal and this evil must be destroyed…forever."

He walks away.

VICTOR'S BEDROOM
Night

He catches sight of himself in the mirror: haggard, drawn. He turns away and staggers to the canopied bed, where he collapses, exhausted, weeping, drawing the curtains.

Victor wakes with a start in the small hours. Rain on the roof. The garret is empty, the chains swinging slightly.

Back to Victor: asleep again, wrestling with troubled dreams. Camera pushes slowly in on Victor, moving into closeup. He is sleeping. Unaware.

A beat. His eyes fly open. An intake of breath. He is paralyzed, feeling the shadow. Working himself up to something—perhaps a scream. He can stand it no longer, thrusts out his arm, jerks the curtain aside—

—and…nothing! Victor sighs with relief. He's overworked, exhausted. He lies back down and looks over—

—and the Creature is there. Looming like a spectre of death. Naked. Beseeching. And we catch our first real glimpse of the Creature's face and body. We see a huge and powerful arm (its left) and an equally powerful leg (its right), which together make for a bizarre mismatch.

Everywhere we look on its body we see bunched and twisted flesh hoisted and held in place

It was on a dreary night of November, that I beheld the accomplishment of my toils. With an anxiety that almost amounted to agony, I collected the instruments of life around me, that I might infuse a spark of being into the lifeless thing that lay at my feet. It was already one in the morning; the rain pattered dismally against the panes, and my candle was nearly burnt out, when, by the glimmer of the half-extinguished light, I saw the dull yellow eye of the creature open; it breathed hard, and a convulsive motion agitated its limbs.

How can I describe my emotions at this catastrophe, or how delineate the wretch whom with such infinite pains and care I had endeavoured to form? His limbs were in proportion, and I had selected his features as beautiful. Beautiful?— Great God! His yellow skin scarcely covered the work of muscles and arteries beneath; his hair was of a lustrous black, and flowing; his teeth of a pearly whiteness; but these luxuriances only formed a more horrid contrast with his watery eyes, that seemed almost the same colour as the dun white sockets in which they were set, his shrivelled complexion, and straight black lips.

by crude stitches. It is as though someone has been hung up by barbed wire. The effect is at once grotesque and pitiable.

VICTOR

No!

Victor lurches from the bed, careening out into the lab. The Creature, unsteady for a moment, then follows him with surprising speed.

VICTOR'S GARRET, LABORATORY
Night

Superimposition: Over the following scene is a closeup of Professor Krempe and the following voice-over.

KREMPE (V.O.)

You fool, Victor Frankenstein of Geneva, how could you know what you had unleashed? How was it pieced together? With bits of thieves? Bits of murderers? Evil stitched to evil stitched to evil.

God help your loved ones.

Victor races through the lab with the Creature behind, catching up. Victor hurls a shelf full of glass jars in its path and runs on around the water tower, past the smashed shelves.

Victor rips the door open, lunges through, slams it in the Creature's face. The Creature presses against the wood, whimpering. He sinks to the floor. Abandoned, shivering with cold, he sees Victor's greatcoat where it fell. He grabs it and drags it over to him, shrouding itself with the cowl. A jar of liquid falls onto the coat as he pulls it to him.

The Creature instinctively scavenges the floor for something in which to wrap himself for protection from the cold. He finds oily rags, machine coverings. Close cuts as he starts to bind his feet with them.

Outside the boarding house: Victor races in from the storm through another door, carrying a pick axe…only to discover the garret door torn off its hinges. He enters, stunned. The Thing is gone.

Dissolve to:

INGOLSTADT ALLEY
Morning

It's grey and drizzly. Garbage litters the alley. There's a shifting, heaving motion, and rats scatter as the waking Creature peers from beneath the greatcoat, lost and confused.

He scrabbles through the garbage for something to eat. He finds an old piece of meat, chews it ravenously.

A distant clanging is heard, and a death cart clatters past the mouth of the alley, the Driver ringing his bell. The Creature watches, uncomprehending, then presses on…

TOWN SQUARE
Day

…and emerges into the square as angle widens. Activity in the square: People are still leaving the city, though not as many as before. Vendors are calling out, selling food to the people streaming past.

The Creature moves through the square, hooded, unnoticed. People trudge along.

The Creature pauses, sniffing the air. An aroma draws him to a vendor's stand: loaves of bread. He sniffs one, picks it up, bites off a chunk, chews. Another bite.

WOMAN (O.S.)
Here! What do you think you're doing?

The Creature glances up. The Vendor's Wife is too stunned to scream.

The Creature drops the loaf, terrified, and backs away from her, straight into the arms of a Rough Man, who pulls him up by his coat, pulling off the hood.

The Creature whips around, horrified faces on all sides…The Vendor's Wife moves towards him, her knife in her hand.

VENDOR'S WIFE
He's the cholera! He's the one been spreadin' the plague!

The faces turn into an angry mob. As they start to shout, the Creature turns and runs away from them and they start to follow, some picking up sticks and stones.

VENDOR'S WIFE
Get him! Get him!

They follow the Creature down a line of shops in a covered way, all shouting as they go.

A tall shelf-load of tin ladles is in front of him and he smashes straight into it. He falls over with it and the crowd tumbles over themselves in an effort to get at him.

He manages to clamber out of the shelves and runs on through the middle of the market, the crowd in pursuit, hitting him with sticks and throwing stones at him.

He runs till he can go no farther, running into the railings at the end of the street. The crowd moves in, surrounding him.

The Creature turns and faces them, moves over, and upturns a huge cart laden with barrels. It's the kind of cart that even a big dray horse could only pull slowly and with difficulty. Yet the Creature up-ends it with ease, sending out a flood of vegetables into the crowd.

The Creature moves away and then a Man (Mark) runs from the crowd and starts hitting him with a stick. The Creature cowers but then pushes him off, propelling him with unbelievable force through the crowd and against a drinking fountain. He knocks the shield off it and drops down into the water below—the Man is killed instantly.

The Other Man (Paul) runs towards the Creature. The Creature picks up the man, throwing him onto his back and then throws him into the crowd, felling several people at once.

He makes good his escape but still the mob streams after him, hurling rocks and sticks. The Rough Man and Woman watch him, letting him go.

VARIOUS STREETS AND ALLEYS
Day

The Creature turns a corner and collapses against a wall to catch his breath. He can hear them coming, shouting.

Suddenly he starts, frightened by a pile of corpses that have recently been abandoned on the steps at his feet. He bends down and picks up a bundle of clothes and runs on up the steps.

Appearing on the other side of the wall, on the steps, he sees a death cart heaped with bodies ap-proaching. He conceals himself from the Driver and then hurls himself down onto the cart to hide himself among the corpses. This is the only way out of the gates during the quarantine.

ROAD AND WOODS OUTSIDE INGOLSTADT
Day

The death cart rattles along the road. The Creature crawls out from under a pile of corpses and tumbles off the back of the cart onto the muddy road. As the cart trundles away, he picks himself up, carrying some clothes, and heads off into the woods.

Dissolve into a beautiful shot of the Creature wading across a river.

Dissolve to:

VICTOR'S GARRET, BEDROOM
Day

Closeup of Victor as his eyes open. Henry is feeding him soup.

HENRY
There now. *(Victor takes a sip)* Rest easy.

Victor is delirious.

VICTOR
Henry, you're here.

Henry laughs gently.

HENRY
Of course *I'm* here. It was touch and go with you, though. Just a bit more.
(offering soup)
I feared cholera. Turned out to be pneumonia.

Victor looks at him.

HENRY
(as he mops Victor's brow with a cool cloth)
Yes, I've become something of a doctor. Even Krempe seems pleased with me. At this rate I might even pass anatomy.

VICTOR
The epidemic?

HENRY
It's dreadful. There is nothing we can do for them. The vulnerable, anyone without food or shelter— the newborn especially—will die.

VICTOR
Are you sure?

HENRY

I'm certain of it.

VICTOR *(whispered)*

Thank God.

HENRY *(perplexed)*

What do you mean?

VICTOR

Nothing.

HENRY

Well, then…that's my shift finished. I'll see you later.

Victor breathes a sigh of relief. Henry goes, leaving Victor alone. Victor hears piano music, gentle, soothing. Is it his delirium? Then it dawns. No, it's real. Victor gets out of bed unsteadily, searching for the music's source.

He moves to the bedroom door and sees that his scientific equipment has been packed up into trunks. The music swells as he searches for it. Mounting intensity. Then he sees her sitting at the piano at the far end of the garret: Elizabeth!

On Victor: his utter joy and happiness.

VICTOR *(overjoyed)*

Elizabeth! *Elizabeth!*

Elizabeth turns and sees Victor, rises from the piano, and starts to run to him.

Victor tries to run to her as fast as his unsteady legs can carry him. When they meet, he all but collapses into her arms. Kissing, touching, holding. They are young animals, children.

VICTOR *(passionate)*

Elizabeth. I thought I'd never see you again.

ELIZABETH *(with great emotion)*

Sshhh. It's all right, it's all right…

VICTOR

Please forgive me, please.

ELIZABETH

Of course I do.

VICTOR

I'm so sorry.

He kisses her passionately. She cradles his head in her hands as they sink onto their knees.

ELIZABETH *(urgent, through tears)*

Victor, I don't know what you were working on… I don't want to know—but it nearly killed you.

VICTOR

It's over. It's finished. It should never have been started. But it's over now. *It's dead.*

They embrace tenderly. Weeping and laughing in
relief all the while.

Dissolve to:

WOODS
Day into dusk

Tilt up to reveal a solitary figure in a greatcoat
trudging through some woods under a darkening
sky. Cold, hungry, wet, tired; carrying his bundle of
clothes.

The Creature pauses, hearing faint music on
the breeze: the sound of a recorder. He turns
around, looking to see where the music comes from
in the woodland. Then he moves off towards the
music…

COTTAGE
Dusk

The Creature approaches cautiously. He eases to a
window, catches a glimpse inside, draws back,
listening. The tune ends. We hear the murmur of
voices and then footsteps clumping across the floor.

The Creature reels back and dives around the
side of the house as the door opens. Felix exits, a
poor, painfully undernourished young man who
works on the land. He heads in the same direction
as the Creature and walks around the corner of the
house just as the Creature scrambles to reach a
small door to a pigsty.

The Creature manages to open the door and
go inside the pigsty as Felix rounds the corner and
follows him inside.

PIGSTY AND COTTAGE
Dusk

The Creature finds himself in the company of pigs. The animals grunt and squeal in alarm.

FELIX (O.S.)
Go on now…Come on.

The Creature scurries farther back into the shadows as Felix comes in. He upends the pail and slop pours into the trough. As Felix goes out, the pigs scurry to eat. The Creature leans forward intently. Food?

He crawls to the trough and squeezes in among the pigs. They jostle, but he jostles right back and laps up the slop with his fingers.

Inside the cottage, the children, Maggie and Thomas, ages 6 and 8, are preparing the table for dinner. Felix's wife, Marie, helps Felix to clean his bleeding hands. The family's evening ritual.

MARIE
How are the pigs?

FELIX
They're happy. They have been fed.

MARIE
How are your hands?

FELIX
They are bleeding again.

On the Creature: He hears Marie humming. He follows the music, crawling back into the darkest recesses where the sty adjoins the wall of the house. Wiping his mouth, he places his eye to a chink between the logs…and sees Grandfather stirring a pot of soup.

The Creature shifts for another view, excited by the sight of them.

Grandfather senses someone's presence. He

pauses to gaze blindly toward the wall, then decides it was probably nothing.

GRANDFATHER
Soup's ready.

THOMAS
Come and sit down, Grandpa.

He lets the children lead him toward the table. Marie brings the pot from the stove.

The Creature eases back to the chink in the wall and sits down. Feeling something in his pocket, he takes out the journal, looks through it—but, not understanding what is written inside, he puts it aside and lies down to sleep.

Dissolve to:

PIGSTY AND COTTAGE
Day

The Creature wakes up amongst the pigs. He rouses, scattering them, and crawls to the slats to look out.

We see Felix returning from the fields with a basket on his back. Although tired, he stops for a moment to pluck a small alpine flower.

The Creature moves to see Felix enter the house and dump the basket out for Marie. There are only a few potatoes and turnips.

FELIX
We'll never get through the winter with this yield. The ground's frozen hard.

MARIE *(standing up)*
We'll have to sell another pig at market.

FELIX *(moving to sit)*
We can't. Not until they lift the quarantine. Even then, it's one less for us. And there's last month's rent. He'll be back for that soon…

MARIE *(sitting beside him)*
Come on, we'll do this together.

FELIX
You're right. We've got to before the snow comes.

A tender moment. He gives her the flower that he picked earlier. She kisses him in thanks.
The Creature watches, deeply moved by them.

MARIE
Come on, then.

They stand and move out.
The Creature reaches through the slats and picks up a potato, sniffs at it.

FIELD NEAR COTTAGE
Day

Felix is hacking furiously at the ground. Marie struggles with a shovel. The ground is covered in a hard frost.

FELIX *(desperate)*
The ground's frozen solid. We haven't the strength to do this. We'd need twenty men to work this field. It's useless.

Marie stops working.

MARIE *(weary)*
We should stop now. It's getting late.

FELIX
We don't have enough to eat.

MARIE *(softly)*
We'll manage. Let's go.

They pick up their near-empty baskets and start to walk up the field and towards home, their arms around each other.

Later that night, out in the field, we find the Creature hacking away at the soil.
At dawn the next day, outside the cottage, all the baskets from the tool shed are now stacked to overflowing before the door. Felix and Marie come out and gaze in wonder.

FELIX
Look, look.

Felix and Marie embrace in joyous amazement.
We move in on the slat of the sty to see the Creature peering out.

That night, warm light spills through the chink in the wall as the Creature peers through. Inside, the family is enjoying a much more generous meal than their last one. The talk is brisk.

GRANDFATHER
…they must be gifts from the Good Spirit of the Forest.

FELIX
Father, nothing in this life comes free of cost. I would like to know who and why.

MAGGIE
Was it, Grandpa? Was it the Good Spirit?

GRANDFATHER
I believe it was.

I discovered also another means through which I was enabled to assist their labours. I found that the youth spent a great part of each day in collecting wood for the family fire; and, during the night, I often took his tools, the use of which I quickly discovered, and brought home firing sufficient for the consumption of several days.

94

FELIX

Will you stop filling their heads with nonsense?

The Creature smiles to himself, knowing he has made life easier.

POND NEAR COTTAGE
Dusk

Grandfather sits playing his recorder. The Creature creeps into view, listening to the music. Grandfather senses his presence and turns as the Creature runs.

GRANDFATHER

Who's there? Felix? Children?

No response. He turns back. Unsettled, he gets up off his log, takes his stick off the tree, and walks away.

PIGSTY AND HOUSE
Night

Marie is writing the word "friend" in chalk on a slate board. She puts the board on the table and turns to Maggie, next to her.

MARIE

Right. What's this one.

MAGGIE
…ff…reh…nn…nd. Friend?

MARIE *(hugging her)*

Friend! Well done.

Inside the pigsty at his slat.

CREATURE *(picking a stitch)*
…freh…nnn…nd. Freehhnnnd.

WOODS NEAR COTTAGE

That night, in the woods, the Creature walks along, muttering:

CREATURE

Friend…Faamilly…Family…Farrtherr…Father.

VICTOR'S GARRET
Day

Victor is packing, checking that the cases holding his equipment are secure, giving orders to a servant. He is intent, determined. The cases are marked "Frankenstein, Geneva."

VICTOR *(to the servant)*
Now this is very important. You must travel with them the entire journey. This equipment must not be left unattended.

SERVANT
Yes, sir.

VICTOR
My father will personally take delivery of them at Geneva. Do you understand?

SERVANT
I do, sir.

VICTOR
Good. Thank you.

HENRY *(coming in)*
Going somewhere?

VICTOR (O.S.)
Yes.

ELIZABETH *(rushing across)*
Henry, look at the locket Victor gave me, isn't it beautiful?

HENRY *(examining it)*
Yes, it's lovely.
(to Victor)
Is this really you?

VICTOR *(moving to him)*
Bad likeness. But for now it'll serve instead of a ring.

HENRY *(embracing him)*
Congratulations on the entirely expected. When, may I ask?

ELIZABETH *(embracing them)*
As soon as we get home. I can't believe we'll be there for New Year's Eve. Victor is going to take over Father's practice.

VICTOR
And expand it.

ELIZABETH *(moving away)*
I'm going ahead now that the quarantine's been lifted. There's so much to do for the wedding.

VICTOR *(to Henry)*
Now the practice needs a partner. There's not much money. But there's food, board and some very good company. It's the ideal position for somebody who's finally passed anatomy. And so, we were wondering if there was anyone you could recommend.

HENRY *(deeply moved)*
Victor, I…don't know what to say…

VICTOR
Well, please say yes.

HENRY
Yes.

ELIZABETH
Yes!

Elizabeth throws a handful of feathers at Henry and he throws feathers back at her and Victor, laughingly saying, "Yes! Yes! Yes!" and Henry and Elizabeth run out of the garret. Henry calls back:

HENRY
And you can write that down in your journal.

On Victor: His reaction to being reminded about the journal.

PIGSTY AND COTTAGE
Night

Holding on the closed journal. Slowly the Creature opens the journal and turns the pages until he reaches a page with the words. He runs his index finger across the words as he reads:

CREATURE
"This is the journal of Victor Frankenstein of Geneva."

A night soon after. Outside the cottage, white flakes drift magically down. The door flies open, and the children pour out. The adults appear in the doorway.

The children set something out in the snow. They call out into the darkness:

MAGGIE/THOMAS
Merry Christmas!

FELIX
Come on, time for bed.

The door closes. The Creature creeps from his sty and scurries closer to investigate. He finds a covered plate. The slate board is jammed in the snow. On it is chalked a child's rendering of a glowing angel and a message:

"For the…Goood Spirr-rit…of the…Forr-rest."

He picks up the plate and uncovers it to see a red silk flower and a wonderful array of Christmas cookies. He sniffs the flower and the cookies and then hurries back with them towards his sty.

Cut to: The next morning, close on Maggie.

MAGGIE
Are you the Good Spirit of the Forest?

Maggie's P.O.V.: the shadowy outline of a large man.

LANDLORD
Not exactly. Where's your father?

Maggie doesn't reply. The Landlord bends down and grabs her face. Maggie squeals in pain.

LANDLORD *(continued)*
I said, where's your father?

Grandfather appears at the door, roused by Maggie's cry. The Landlord, seeing him, relaxes his grip on Maggie, who darts off into the woods, calling for her Mother.

GRANDFATHER
Who's there? Maggie!

LANDLORD

No!

Grandfather stands listening intently as the Landlord trudges up to him. Grandfather recognizes the step.

GRANDFATHER (*continued, defiant*)
Oh, it's *you*. What have you done to Maggie!

LANDLORD
Is he in there? Hiding behind a blind old man?

Grandfather advances on the Landlord, wildly brandishing his cane at him.

GRANDFATHER
Get away!

The Landlord steps behind Grandfather and trips him up. Grandfather plunges into the snow face first.

LANDLORD (*jabbing the cane into his back*)
Don't blame me. Blame your son for not paying his rent on time!

The Landlord swipes at the head of the snowman and turns to enter the house, but stops dead in his tracks.

The doorway is filled by the massive frame of the Creature. The Landlord looks up at the Creature, paralyzed with terror. The Creature lifts the Landlord into the air and pushes his head through the porch thatch, and then flings him like a rag doll into the snow.

Grandfather starts to get to his feet.

WOODS NEAR COTTAGE
Day

Felix is laying traps. Marie and Thomas are collecting berries and placing them in their baskets.

A scream echoes across the countryside. Felix turns from laying traps. Marie stops what she is doing and moves to Felix. Softly:

FELIX (*terrified*)
My God. No.

They start to run off towards the house.

COTTAGE
Day

Grandfather, still breathless after his ordeal, is standing in the cottage by the fire. The Creature stands on the steps outside.

GRANDFATHER
Thank you, my friend, thank you so much. Won't you come and sit by the fire? Please?

Grandfather slowly sits down. The Creature doesn't move.

GRANDFATHER (continued)
Don't be afraid. Come and warm yourself. Please come in. There's only me here, come in…

Cut to: Maggie running through the woods.

The Creature slowly comes in and sits facing him.

GRANDFATHER (continued)
That's better. I'm glad you finally came in. A man shouldn't have to hide in the shadows.

CREATURE
Better that way…for me.

GRANDFATHER
Why?

CREATURE
…People are afraid. Except…except you.

GRANDFATHER (smiles)
It can't be as bad as that.

CREATURE (soft)
Worse.

GRANDFATHER
I can see you with my hands. If you'll trust me.

The Creature decides to trust. He eases forward. Grandfather runs his fingers over his features.

Out in the woods, Maggie runs into the arms of Felix.

MAGGIE (wailing)
Papa! Papa! He hurt Grandpa!

Felix, Marie, and Thomas all speaking at once: "Who hurt Grandpa! What was that noise? Tell me what that noise was!
Back to the cottage: the Creature and Grandfather.

GRANDFATHER (taking his hand)
You poor man. Have you no friends?

CREATURE
There are some people, but they don't know me.

GRANDFATHER
Why do you not go to them?

The Creature pauses. Emotions swirling.

CREATURE

Because…I am so very…ugly…and they are so
very…beautiful.

And the family suddenly arrives. The Creature
turns to them, but Felix grabs a poker and rushes
at him, hitting him across the back. The Creature
tries to move away.

FELIX *(screams)*

Father!
(to Creature)
Get out! You're a monster, get out!

CREATURE

No!

The children and Marie rush to Grandfather as Felix
continues beating the Creature around the room.

GRANDFATHER *(standing up)*
Leave him alone! No, leave him!

The Creature is screaming and taking the blows,
writhing in agony, the children hiding behind their
Grandfather, the old man dazed and shouting,
Marie tugging on his arm. The Creature rolls from
under the brutal beating and sails out the door.
    Felix turns from the door.

FELIX
We have to leave here! Now!

WOODS NEAR COTTAGE
Day

Closeup on the Creature leaning against a tree, his
head bowed with misery, weeping, trying to catch
his breath. He sinks to his knees, hands clutched to
his chest. Then he pulls the little red silk flower
from the cuff of his coat. It lies glittering in his
huge, misshapen palm. He runs off.

COTTAGE
Day

The sky is brewing as the Creature runs across the

I continued for the remainder of the day in my hovel in a state of utter and stupid despair. My protectors had departed, and had broken the only link that held me to the world. For the first time the feelings of revenge and hatred filled my bosom, and I did not strive to control them; but, allowing myself to be borne away by the stream, I bent my mind towards injury and death. When I thought of my friends…these thoughts vanished, and a gush of tears somewhat soothed me. But again, when I reflected that they had spurned and deserted me, anger returned, a rage of anger; and, unable to injure any thing human, I turned my fury towards inanimate objects. As night advanced, I placed a variety of combustibles around the cottage; and, after having destroyed every vestige of cultivation in the garden, I waited with forced impatience until the moon had sunk to commence my operations.

As the night advanced, a fierce wind arose from the wood, and quickly dispersed the clouds that had loitered in the heavens: the blast tore along like a mighty avalanche, and produced a kind of insanity in my spirits, that burst all bounds of reason and reflection. I lighted the dry branch of a tree, and danced with fury around the devoted cottage, my eyes still fixed on the western horizon, the edge of which the moon nearly touched. A part of its orb was at length hid, and I waved my brand; it sunk, and, with a loud scream, I fired the straw, and heath, and bushes, which I had collected. The wind fanned the fire, and the cottage was quickly enveloped by the flames, which clung to it, and licked it with their forked and destroying tongues.

As soon as I was convinced that no assistance could save any part of the habitation, I quitted the scene, and sought for refuge in the woods.

courtyard toward the house, breathless, holding his palm out.

Nothing. No people, no animals. The Creature's eyes go wide. He dashes to the house—

—and stops in the doorway. The room is empty. Items have been scattered and left behind. Books, clothes, even the old man's recorder. They left in a hurry.

CREATURE
No…no…

He is devastated. Then he thinks of something and moves out.

Outside, he races into the sty and grabs the journal. With mounting panic he turns the pages and discovers his own likeness: it's Victor's sketch of his "patchwork man." The Creature gazes for a long time, his eyes going wider, revelation slowly dawning.

VICTOR (V.O.)
"Massive birth defects. Greatly enhanced physical strength but the resulting re-animant is malfunctional and pitiful and dead. These experiments are at an end."

…and he drops the journal, clawing at his coat in a surge of panic, wrenching it open to reveal his chest—and the massive suture scars down his torso, an exact match of the drawing. He throws his head back in an animalistic primal scream.

Cut to:

Creature's hand holding a lit torch, setting a pile of furniture alight. Flames rise within the cottage.

The Creature stands outside the hovel, watching as the flames get higher. The house is being completely consumed by the fire.

He slowly turns to face the camera, raises his arms and head to the sky, and shouts:

CREATURE
I will take revenge on you, Frankenstein!

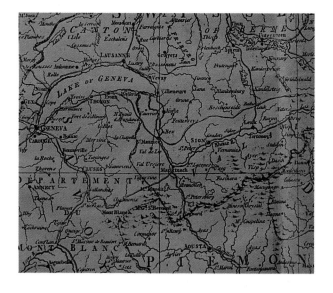

MONT BLANC
Day

The Alps. Angle widens to reveal a lone, windswept figure traversing the glacier, greatcoat billowing in the wind.

The Creature rises from below a crest and gazes down, glowering.

CREATURE *(savagely)*

Geneva.

Dissolve to:

FRANKENSTEIN MANSION
Day

A carriage is driving up to the mansion. As it stops in front, the mansion doors open and William and the family pour out.

FATHER
Quickly.

WILLIAM *(running down steps)*
She's here! She's here! We got your letter! We got your letter! It's the first one I was allowed to read.

Elizabeth picks him up and hugs him.

FATHER
It's wonderful news, my dear.

JUSTINE
Congratulations, Elizabeth. I'm happy for you.

ELIZABETH
Thank you, Justine.

JUSTINE
Is that the locket?

MRS. MORITZ
Congratulations.

ELIZABETH
Thank you, Mrs. Moritz.

JUSTINE *(showing William)*
Look how handsome Victor is.

WILLIAM *(taking the locket)*
Elizabeth? Can I take this to show Peter?

ELIZABETH *(a gentle reproof)*
Willie, it's not a toy.

But William is already tearing off down the lawn.

FATHER *(indulgent)*
Oh, let him go.
(shouting to William)
William, don't dawdle! William!

William runs on down the drive as the carriage pulls away, heading into the miles of wooded acreage behind the house. His favorite shortcut.

MANSION GRAND BALLROOM
Late Day

The room is bustling with activity. In a riot of white silks and laces, Elizabeth stands on a table before a huge mirror as she is fitted for her wedding dress. Justine and Mrs. Moritz are kneeling on the table

And now I must tell you a little story that will please, and perhaps amuse you. Do you not remember Justine Moritz? Probably you do not; I will relate her history, therefore, in a few words. Madame Moritz, her mother, was a widow with four children, of whom Justine was the third. This girl had always been the favourite of her father; but, through a strange perversity, her mother could not endure her, and, after the death of M. Moritz, treated her very ill. My aunt observed this; and, when Justine was twelve years of age, prevailed on her mother to allow her to live at her house....

~

I must say also a few words to you, my dear cousin, of little darling William. I wish you could see him; he is very tall of his age, with sweet laughing blue eyes, dark eye-lashes, and curling hair. When he smiles, two little dimples appear on each cheek, which are rosey with health. He has already had one or two little wives, but Louisa Biron is his favourite, a pretty little girl of five years of age.

[*letter from Elizabeth to Victor*]

sewing a part of the train, working urgently but laughing. Justine is wielding a needle and thread while Mrs. Moritz holds the fabric steady. Justine looks up at Elizabeth, and in a momentary loss of concentration, she drives the needle into Mrs. Moritz's thumb.

MRS. MORITZ *(brutal)*
Justine, you idiot! Pay attention! Anyone would think that you're the one who's getting married!

JUSTINE *(tight)*
Yes, Mother.

ELIZABETH
What's wrong?

JUSTINE *(even tighter)*
Nothing.

Justine sees genuine concern. She softens:

JUSTINE *(continued)*
Really.

MRS. MORITZ
Just leave it. You've ruined it now.

Justine turns away, upset.

COUNTRYSIDE
Late Day

William hurries and dawdles along as kids do, the precious locket clutched in his hands, admiring it. He pauses, hearing faint tones carried on the breeze, eerie and flutelike: a recorder. He follows the sounds further into the woods.

Cut to:

COUNTRYSIDE, POND
Late Day

William comes into view of the pond. There's a figure sitting half-concealed among the tall reeds, gazing off across the water and playing his delicate wind instrument with oddly pleasing dissonance (again, a simple variation of our familiar "Waltz/ Love Theme").

William draws close, curious, not wanting to intrude but listening to the music. The figure in the reeds still hasn't noticed him…

…and then his head abruptly whips around. They stare at each other for a moment. The Creature smiles at the little boy. Then William's eyes go wide. The boy turns and runs as the monster in the reeds lunges to its feet.

The boy keeps running. The Creature comes shambling up from the pond and sees something lying in the grass. He picks up the dropped object.

As he rises, he finds himself staring at the locket. At the small painting it contains: of Victor. He raises his gaze after the fleeing boy.

CREATURE
Frankenstein…

MANSION GRAND BALLROOM
Late Day

Elizabeth and Mrs. Moritz fitting Elizabeth's dress. Justine stands apart and alone. Father enters with Claude. Both men are worried.

CLAUDE *(to footmen)*
You, with me.

FATHER
Elizabeth, have you seen Willie?

ELIZABETH
Isn't he back yet?

FATHER
Claude rode over there to see if he'd lost track of time. They say he never arrived.

ELIZABETH
It's far too late for him to still be out.

She follows Father out. Justine watches, and then follows too.

COUNTRYSIDE, WOODS
Late Day

A massive search is in progress. People are scouring the fields on horse and on foot, shouting William's name.

CLAUDE

William!…Everybody spread out…some of you go and check by the bridge.

Elizabeth enters frame, calling out:

ELIZABETH

Willie!

Cut to: Establishing shot of lightning in the sky.

In another part of the woods we find: Justine, alone, angry, pacing the woods, anxious and upset.

JUSTINE

Willie! This isn't a game! Willie!

COUNTRYSIDE, BARN
Night

Establishing shot of a barn, lashed by rain and lightning. Thunder can be heard in the distance. A storm approaching.

JUSTINE

We're all so tired. I'm so tired.

Justine walks up to the barn, exhausted.

JUSTINE

It's so late.

She walks into the barn.

Cut to: Victor and Henry arriving at mansion.

MANSION ENTRANCE
Late Day

Mrs. Moritz helps Father up towards the house as Victor and Henry ride up on horses.

VICTOR *(warmly)*

Father…I'm so pleased to see you.

He gets off his horse and then sees Father taking off his wig. The look on his face tells the story.

VICTOR *(continued)*

What's wrong?

Inside the barn, Justine is asleep in the hay, haggard, wet, exhausted. The Creature looms over her, a monstrous shape backlit by the lightning, gazing on her beauty. His hand reaches down, hovering

reverently, wishing to caress the swell of her breasts at the neckline of her bodice…Instead he gently lays the locket on her bodice and moves away.

FRANKENSTEIN MANSION
Night

A driving rain. Victor and Henry rush toward Father and Mrs. Moritz at the front of the house.

VICTOR
I've checked the East Ridge. There's nothing there.

Suddenly through the gloom they see:
    Elizabeth, with only a cloak thrown over her silken underwear, emerges from the woods and stands in the downpour at the far edge of the lawn. Flashes of lightning intermittently reveal her, drenched and weeping. She is holding William in her arms. The boy's arms hang limp, his head dangles back.

VICTOR
Elizabeth? Elizabeth…

ELIZABETH *(sobbing)*
I found him…I found him…

Victor starts to run towards her, Henry, Mrs. Moritz, and Father following across the lawn.

109

FATHER

Nooooo!

Elizabeth staggers towards them.

Victor reaches her first as the others crowd around, crushing and jostling as she collapses into Victor's arms, cradling William to the ground—

—and then Father is there, shoving his way through, seeing his dead boy and collapsing in the muck with a scream. Henry and Mrs. Moritz, Claude and the other servants all gather around.

Smash cut to: Establishing shot, mansion exterior.

MANSION BEDROOM
Daybreak

We see Willie lying on a table. He is dead. A cover is draped over him.

In Father's bedroom: silence. All we hear now is the soft ticking of a clock.

Henry tenderly ministers to Father, who lies gravely ill. He is muttering incoherently.

HENRY

We did everything we could, sir. Rest now, just rest now. We did everything we could…

Downstairs in the parlor, Elizabeth is sitting with elbows crossed, holding herself together, face ashen. She is dazed, still in shock. Victor stands beside her. Henry now comes down the stairs behind them.

Mrs. Moritz is nearby, looking much the same. Her eyes swim with tears.

MRS. MORITZ *(to Victor, in a torrent)*

Sir. I'm terrified for my girl. She's still out looking for William. We parted badly, you see. I was cruel to her. I didn't mean it. I think she finds it very hard now, with your wedding. She loves you dearly. I couldn't bear it if anything happened to her. She's all I've got. Please help me…

VICTOR *(softly)*

We'll organize another search now that it's light. We'll find her, Mrs. Moritz, I promise.

Henry stands next to Victor. They confer in whispers. Elizabeth turns to them.

ELIZABETH
How is Father?

HENRY
His heart is breaking.

She turns away. There is a knock at the door. Victor goes to answer it.

At the entryway, a footman opens the door. A Militiaman hovers outside, his face grim.

MILITIAMAN
Mr. Frankenstein. We've apprehended the murderer. Not five miles from here, hiding in a barn.
(producing the locket)
We found this on her. It is yours, I believe, sir? Sir, you must come immediately, the townspeople have gone mad…

TOWN SQUARE
Morning

Victor, Elizabeth, and the Militiaman run into the town square. The crowd rushes past them.

ELIZABETH
My God, what are they doing?

VICTOR
For God's sake, man, can't you stop this?

MILITIAMAN
They've gone wild. This is a lynching mob.

Suddenly they see: A doorway as the door flies open and a crowd of men surges through, dragging Justine. The Family Minister is with her.

MINISTER
Stop! This is unlawful.

ELIZABETH/VICTOR
Justine!!

They run off towards her.

A crowd of angry people mobs them. Justine is picked up and carried above the crowd. Shouts of "child killer!"

As Justine is dragged along, the crowd fighting to get at her, Victor and Elizabeth run alongside, trying to get near her.

VICTOR (bellowing)
Justine!

Justine sees Victor:

JUSTINE (pleading, sobbing)
Victor! Help me! I was trying to find him. I went to

111

the lake, but it was dark. I wanted to bring him to you—he must be there for the wedding. He's so tiny…I'm sorry.

The mob drags her off up some narrow steps in the wall. Victor, Elizabeth, and the crowd move off to see—
    —Justine appear at the top of the wall. Screaming and fighting with the men, she is pushed to her knees and a noose placed around her neck.
    Mrs. Moritz and Claude run into the square.
    Victor and Elizabeth look on to see: a group of men on top of the high wall pull Justine to her feet and throw her off.

VICTOR/ELIZABETH

No!!

A pair of feet drop heavily in frame. Thump-crack!
    Victor stands and stares in horror, then starts to pull Elizabeth away as Claude and Mrs. Moritz fight their way through the crowd to reach Justine's body.

The crowd cheers and starts to throw stones at it and them.

FRANKENSTEIN MANSION
Night

A storm is gathering. Lightning flashes and distant thunder can be heard. Victor crosses the grass.

VICTOR

Claude…

CLAUDE

We have cut her down, sir. We can bury her in the morning.

VICTOR

Thank you, Claude. Get to bed.

Victor moves on towards the house when—
    —a giant hand thrusts into frame and grabs his shoulder.

Victor whirls—a flash of lightning—and he is staring up into the Creature's face. He is transfixed in horror. Softly:

CREATURE *(raising his arm)*
I will meet you there—on the sea of ice.

Lightning dances in the sky, illuminating Mont Blanc with a crackling halo of electricity…

…and then the Creature vanishes. Victor falls, gasping.

VICTOR
Oh, God. Justine. Forgive me.

FRANKENSTEIN MANSION
Day

Close on the spinning drum of a handgun, its metalwork glinting in the sunlight.

We see Victor marching across the lawn, flanked by Elizabeth and Henry. They mask their anxiety with a show of firmness.

ELIZABETH
Victor, tell me who this man is? How do you know he's responsible?

VICTOR *(impatient, distracted)*
I will tell you everything after I've destroyed him.

HENRY
If what you say is true, then surely this is a matter for the police.

VICTOR
They wouldn't understand.

Victor marches away from them towards his horse.

ELIZABETH *(exasperated)*
Well, neither do I.

Victor, now on his horse, turns to Elizabeth.

VICTOR
Then just accept it.

113

Oh, Frankenstein, be not equitable to every other, and trample upon me alone, to whom thy justice, and even thy clemency and affection, is most due. Remember, that I am thy creature: I ought to be thy Adam; but I am rather the fallen angel, whom thou drivest from joy for no misdeed. Every where I see bliss, from which I alone am irrevocably excluded. I was benevolent and good; misery made me a fiend. Make me happy, and I shall again be virtuous.

Victor rides off, leaving Elizabeth stung to the marrow.

MONT BLANC
Day

From high above, we see Victor trudging his way up the mountain. His horse has been abandoned in the foothills. He pauses for a moment to catch his breath, and moves on.

Farther up the glacier, Victor climbs on up, his pickaxe in his hand. He stops and looks around— no sign of his adversary—and climbs on up the jagged wall of the glacier.

He looks madly around and then above him and behind him. As if from nowhere, the Creature leaps towards him.

Victor turns to face him and as the Creature lands, he pushes Victor away and into the air. Victor flies through the air, landing in the snow. He tumbles down a steep slope…

…and on down another slope and, continuing to fall, disappears into a crevice…

ICE CAVE
Day

…and down a tunnel to land in a misty pool in an ice cave. He is knocked out by the fall. The Creature moves towards the unconscious Victor and drags him out of the pool to safety.

Some time later, Victor wakes up, looks around, and finds himself being watched by the Creature, who sits on the far side of a fire from him.

CREATURE
Come warm yourself if you like.

VICTOR
You speak.

CREATURE
Yes, I speak. And read. And think…and know the ways of Man. *(pause)*

VICTOR *(moves forward)*
How did you find me?

The Creature turns towards the books beside him.

CREATURE
Your journal.

Victor sits down.

VICTOR
You mean to kill me?

CREATURE
No.

VICTOR
You murdered my brother, didn't you?

CREATURE
Do you think I am evil?

CREATURE *(continued)*
Do you think the dying cries of your brother were music in my ears?

He raises his hand before Victor's eyes, bony fingers curling to clutch an invisible throat.

CREATURE (continued)

I took him by the throat with one hand…lifted him off the ground…and slowly crushed his neck. *(emotion growing)*
And as I killed him, I saw your face.

Victor stares in horror as the Creature relates his story with tears shining in his monstrous eyes.

CREATURE (continued)

You gave me these emotions, but you didn't tell me how to use them. Now two people are dead. Because of us.

Victor is crushed by remorse. A sob escapes him.

CREATURE (continued)

Why?

VICTOR

There was something at work in my soul which I do not understand.

CREATURE

What of my soul? Do I have one? Or was that a part you left out?

Who were these people of which I am comprised? Good people? Bad people?

VICTOR

Materials. Nothing more.

CREATURE

You're wrong. *(picks up the recorder)* Do you know I knew how to play this?

He puts down the recorder.

CREATURE (continued)

In which part of me did this knowledge reside? In these hands? In this mind? In this heart? *(beat)*
And reading and speaking. Not things learned… so much as things remembered.

VICTOR

Trace memories in the brain, perhaps.

CREATURE
Did you ever consider the consequences of your actions? *(beat)* You gave me life, and then left me to die. *(beat)* Who am I?

VICTOR
…You…I don't know…

CREATURE
And you think I am evil.

VICTOR *(very slowly)*
What can I do?

CREATURE
There is something I want. *(pause)* A friend.

VICTOR
Friend?

CREATURE
A companion. A female. Someone like me, so she won't hate me.

VICTOR *(horrified)*
Like you? Oh, God. You don't know what you're asking.

CREATURE
I do know that for the sympathy of one living being, I would make peace with all…I have love in me the likes of which you can scarcely imagine. And rage the likes of which you would not believe. If I cannot satisfy the one, I will indulge the other.

VICTOR
And if I consent? How will you live?

CREATURE
We'd travel north, my bride and I. To the farthest reaches of the Pole, where no man has ever set foot. There we would live out our lives. Together. No human eye would ever see us again. This I vow. You must help me. Please.

Pushing slowly in on Victor. Considering it. Beaten.

VICTOR

If it is possible to right this wrong…*(beat)*…then I will do it.

FRANKENSTEIN MANSION
Day

Elizabeth rushes across the lawn with Henry and Claude.

ELIZABETH/HENRY/CLAUDE

Victor…Victor…Sir…

ELIZABETH

Are you all right?

Victor dismounts as they approach, hands the reins to the Stable Boy, and embraces Elizabeth tightly.

VICTOR

It's all right. It's all right. I'm safe.

HENRY

What happened?

ELIZABETH

Tell us…tell us, Victor.

But Victor walks on past her and away towards the house.

ELIZABETH *(fiercely)*

Victor, you have to tell us what happened.

MANSION PARLOR
Day

We find them in heated discussion as they rush in.

VICTOR

A month, that's all I ask. And then we can be married and forget this whole business. I promise.

· ELIZABETH *(stops)*

Promise! Promise! Don't dare use that word to me! You promised to tell me who this man was. You promised to abandon this work for good… Your promises don't mean anything.

VICTOR

Elizabeth…

ELIZABETH

I have to leave this house.

> *Like one who, on a lonely road,*
> *Doth walk in fear and dread,*
> *And, having once turn'd round, walks on,*
> *And turns no more his head;*
> *Because he knows a frightful fiend*
> *Doth close behind him tread.*
> Quoted by Mary Shelley
> from Coleridge's *Rime of the Ancient Mariner*

VICTOR

What are you saying? Where will you go?

ELIZABETH

I don't know. Somewhere where I can recover…

VICTOR

This is ridiculous…I haven't got time to argue…

ELIZABETH *(turning to him)*

Isn't it convenient? Doesn't it fit in with your plans? Don't you ever think of anyone or anything but yourself?

She races off up the stairs. Victor turns away.

CREATURE (V.O.)

You must help me…

Cut to:

MANSION ATTIC
Day

Victor moves along the line of packing cases. He stops, looking at a huge box.

VICTOR

God forgive me.

He pulls on a rope, which reveals the gleaming copper of the sarcophagus as it comes out of its box.

Montage:

Victor checks along the line of packing cases, some now partly opened, and up to Claude as he prises off a lid.
    Claude raises the needle board and Victor checks the sharpness.
    They lift a load of galvanic flux jars onto a trestle.

They thread up the rope which runs the Wims-hurst machine.

We follow the body grid along the grill to find Victor checking and adjusting.

The fire is lit under the sarcophagus. Victor dismisses Claude.

Montage:

Elizabeth is packing books into a trunk…
　　Throwing clothes from the wardrobe…
　　Furniture gets covered in sheets.
　　She covers the cherished wedding dress in a black drape.
　　Taking a last look at her room, furniture shrouded in white sheets, she closes the doors…

Cut to:

CEMETERY
Night

Camera drifts among the tombstones to reveal an eerie sight: someone hunched in a grave, digging madly, dirt flying. We hear the thunk of a shovel hitting wood—and the Creature disappears into the grave.

　　The lid is wrenched aside and we see Justine.
　　P.O.V. shifts to the inside of the coffin, so that we see the Creature as if through her eyes. He peers down at us, almost close enough to kiss.

MANSION ATTIC
Morning

The mottled corpse of Justine is uncovered.

　　Victor stares down in utter horror at her cold, dead face, the blue lips already beginning to shrivel, the eyes purple, sunken. Knowing that she loved him. Knowing it's his fault that she's dead. He can barely get the words out:

VICTOR
Why…her?

CREATURE
Materials, remember? Nothing more. Your words.

VICTOR
No.

Victor starts to walk away, but the Creature races after him, grabs him by the throat, and pushes him down on the table where the dead Justine is lying.

CREATURE
You will honor your promise to me!

VICTOR
I will not! Kill me now!

I trembled, and my heart failed within me; when, on looking up, I saw, by the light of the moon, the daemon at the casement. A ghastly grin wrinkled his lips as he gazed on me, where I sat fulfilling the task which he had allotted to me. Yes, he had followed me in my travels; he had loitered in forests, hid himself in caves, or taken refuge in wide and desert heaths; and he now came to mark my progress, and claim the fulfilment of my promise.

As I looked on him, his countenance expressed the utmost extent of malice and treachery. I thought with a sensation of madness on my promise of creating another like to him, and, trembling with passion, tore to pieces the thing on which I was engaged. The wretch saw me destroy the creature on whose future existence he depended for happiness, and, with a howl of devilish despair and revenge, withdrew.

CREATURE

That is mild compared to what will come. If you deny me my wedding night…I will be with you on yours.

Cut to: Victor running down the ballroom stairs, shouting for Elizabeth.

MANSION, GRAND BALLROOM
Morning

Victor runs across the vast ballroom.
    Elizabeth, bags packed, is heading for the door of the chapel. The doors nearest her are locked, and he moves along them trying to get in as he speaks.

VICTOR

Elizabeth! Wait. Wait. Please wait. Please. I have to speak to you. Please.

He comes into the chapel at the altar end and stops.

ELIZABETH

What do you want to say?

VICTOR

Don't go. Please don't go. I'm frightened.

ELIZABETH

Of what?

VICTOR

I have done something so terrible…so evil…and I'm frightened…if I tell you the truth…that I will lose you.

ELIZABETH *(simple)*

You'll lose me if you don't.

VICTOR *(breaking down)*

I don't know what to do.

He sinks down onto his knees. Elizabeth slowly makes her way up the chapel to kneel down facing him.

ELIZABETH

Will you marry me, Victor? *(beat)* Marry me today and tomorrow tell me everything. *(beat)* But you must tell me the truth. Then together we can face anything. Whatever you've done, whatever has happened, I love you.

MANSION, FATHER'S BEDROOM
Day

A small ceremony has been hurriedly organized at Father's bedside. Henry stands as best man. Claude is also present. The Priest faces Victor and Elizabeth.

MINISTER

…to share the truth and the whole truth…for good or ill…to stand by each other in sickness and in health…and in joy, from this day forward till death do you part…

Victor and Elizabeth look at Father, who motions them to kiss, and they do.

MANSION ENTRANCE
Day

Claude is armed with a rifle, ready to pull out. A Stable Hand is walking with Victor.

STABLE HAND
Who is this man, sir? How shall we know him?

VICTOR *(deadly serious)*
Believe me, you'll know him.

CLAUDE
He killed Master William and Justine Moritz died for
it. No hesitation, lads! Shoot the bastard on sight!

Cries of assent. Victor joins Henry and Elizabeth.

VICTOR
Henry…

HENRY
Don't worry about a thing. You two look after each
other. I'll look after your father.

The horses gallop away. Those left behind scatter
across the courtyard. Henry turns and walks back
toward the house. Angle widens and camera cranes
up to reveal the Creature inside the house at the
window of Father's bedroom.
In the bed behind him, the old man stirs. The
Creature turns and walks toward Father.
On Father's face: An expression of horror. He
dies. The Creature reaches down, closes his eyes. A
tender gesture.

WOODS NEAR LAKE GENEVA
Dusk

Victor and Elizabeth riding along with the Guards.
As they approach Lake Geneva, a magnificent
sunset bathes the mountains and storm clouds start
to roll in. A ferry is crossing the lake, moving away
from us, rippling the water.
Tilt down to reveal the ferry dock. Claude rides
up to Victor and Elizabeth, on horseback.

CLAUDE
I'm sorry, sir, the last ferry's gone. There's nothing
now till morning.

VICTOR
Damn!

CLAUDE
I'll ride on ahead and secure you lodging for the
night.

VICTOR
Thank you, Claude.

FISHING LODGE
Night

A big chalet nestled in the woods by the lake. The
storm is raging. Claude and his men are positioned
at the entrances.

VICTOR
Make sure you keep your pistols dry.

GUARD 2
They're dry enough. And if they fail, we've others.
And if those fail…we can always gut the bastard.

CLAUDE
Go to your post…
(to Victor)
Don't worry, sir. You're well guarded. Now why
don't you go upstairs to your wife? It's not often a
man has his wedding night.

Claude winks.

CHALET BRIDAL SUITE
Night

Elizabeth is lighting candles. She turns from the
fireplace as Victor enters to find the room aglow
with dozens of candles.
He takes off his coat, lays down his pistols, and
moves across to her.

ELIZABETH
You're soaking.

VICTOR
I know.

ELIZABETH
Brother and sister no more.

VICTOR
Now husband and wife.

She leans up and gives him a kiss that would melt
glass, triggering the sexiest seduction imaginable…
kissing, caressing, Victor stripping off his shirt, the
camera drifting around them in slow circles, candles spinning like a fever that's been building for
a lifetime.

Slowly he unties the strings on her bodice… turning her…back to him…he kisses her neck… caressing her breasts and feeling between her legs…

…and now onto the magnificent canopied bed. Kneeling together, bodies touching, hands seeking, mouths joining…Elizabeth lying back. Victor sinking down, running his hands up her thighs, making her shudder with desire…and he kneels up to pull on the strings of her bodice while Elizabeth starts to undo the buttons on his breeches…

Then the mournful tones of a recorder reach them. Elizabeth smiles, thinking it's romantic, but Victor freezes at the sound.

ELIZABETH
Victor!

VICTOR
Lock the door!

He picks up his guns and his shirt and leaves.

Outside the chalet, the men converge, shouting in the rain:

GUARD 2
I saw him in a flash of lightning! He vanished toward the lake!

CLAUDE
You two, stay here!

Back to Elizabeth:

Slowly, tensely, she lies back on the bed.

And there, silhouetted above her, hanging atop the bed canopy like a huge black spider is the Creature.

Cut to: Victor and Claude outside.

Cut back to bedroom: Suddenly the Creature's hand tears through the canvas and covers Elizabeth's mouth.

Outside again: Victor and Claude come running back from the lake. They stop before Guard 2:

GUARD 2
We lost him.

Victor's eyes drift up, his breath catching in his throat. The French doors are swaying in the wind.

VICTOR
Elizabeth…

Victor and Claude run towards the chalet.
    Inside the bedroom, Elizabeth watches, transfixed as the Creature, now kneeling, leans down over her. He pauses, stunned at her beauty. A moment passes between them.

CREATURE (O.S.)
Don't bother to scream.

Slowly the Creature takes his hand from her mouth.

ELIZABETH
Please, please don't hurt me.

He stares at her—so close their lips almost touch.

CREATURE
You're more lovely than I ever could have imagined.

She peers at him, trying to understand.
    Footsteps come pounding up the stairs. There is a heavy crash of men throwing their shoulders at the door. Victor bursts through the outside door

and into the corridor to bash against the interior door.

VICTOR (O.S.)

Elizabeth!

…and it all changes in an instant. The Creature cocks his arm back and plunges his fist toward her chest with pile-driver force. She writhes up in agony and falls back dead.

On the landing outside the suite, the men hear her scream cut short. They give one last mighty rush at the door—

—and burst in just in time to see the Creature pull out her heart. He holds it out towards them:

CREATURE

I keep my promises…

He pushes her off the bed onto a table of candles. Close on Elizabeth from behind: her face smashing against the side table as she continues to fall.

Close on Elizabeth: her face smashes into the glass bowl on the side table. Blood everywhere.

Close on Elizabeth's hair: candles spill onto her hair, setting it alight.

Close on Elizabeth: as her head smashes against the hard wooden ridge next to the bed. Blood exploding as she makes impact against it.

The Creature races across the room as the men open fire, shredding the walls to splinters with an explosive fusillade of shots. But the Creature is too fast. He hits the leaded window head-on with the force of an anvil…

View shifts to outside chalet…and he goes sailing out into empty space in a hurricane of shattering glass. He crashes into a low-hanging branch, then drops forty feet to the grass below and vanishes like the breeze.

Inside the suite: Victor rushes to the bed and frantically puts out the burning hair with his hands. He sweeps his limp, murdered bride into his arms, cradling her to his breast, screams trailing off into wracking moans and sobs of despair:

While I still hung over her in the agony of despair, I happened to look up. The windows of the room had before been darkened; and I felt a kind of panic on seeing the pale yellow light of the moon illuminate the chamber. The shutters had been thrown back; and, with a sensation of horror not to be described, I saw at the open window a figure the most hideous and abhorred. A grin was on the face of the monster; he seemed to jeer, as with his fiendish finger he pointed towards the corpse of my wife. I rushed towards the window, and drawing a pistol from my bosom, shot; but he eluded me, leaped from his station, and, running with the swiftness of lightning, plunged into the lake.

VICTOR
Oh, God…

Outside the chalet: Victor carries his dead wife down the steps and through the downpour.

FRANKENSTEIN MANSION
Night

A storm is raging. Lightning hitting the mansion.

We move in quickly towards the house as a horse gallops up to it and veers to a wild stop.

Victor jumps down, gathers up the body, which is wrapped in a red cloak, mounts the steps and slams the large doors behind him.

Inside: Victor charges across the ballroom, heading for the stairs. Henry pursues him, appalled.

HENRY
For God's sake, tell me what happened.

VICTOR
There's no point. I know what I have to do.

HENRY *(panicked realization)*
No, Victor…You can't do this.
(tries to stop him)
I won't let you do this.

VICTOR
She's gone. I love her. What would you do?

HENRY
Leave her in peace.

VICTOR
Peace?…You call this peace? You think my father wouldn't have done this for my mother?

HENRY
Your father's dead.

126

VICTOR
Then, there's nothing left to lose.

HENRY
Nothing but your soul.

Victor carries Elizabeth up the staircase. Her long blood-red cloak trails behind them.

We follow Victor through the upstairs corridor as he continues to carry Elizabeth towards the locked doors of the attic, the lightning flashing around them.

Continuing on up the stairs of the attic, he carries her into the darkened room.

Montage:

...and we launch into the final throbbing madness:

We see Victor taking the covers off his "spare parts" bodies, turning on the generators and Wimshurst machines, heating up the amniotic fluid.

Throwing books off a table and sliding Elizabeth into their place. He turns her over to check her body, then moves over to his tools and picks up a cleaver, taking it over to where she lies.

Victor turns the dead Justine onto her front side and rips the clothes from her body. He takes the meat cleaver and pulls her right hand out as if to chop it clean off.

Victor madly sewing the body parts together as we wildly revolve around him.

He checks his stitches on the face.

He cuts the burnt remains of Elizabeth's lovely hair, clipping and shaving away around the horrible burns.

Seen from above, the body lies on the grid covered by a shroud.

He races across the room—the grid, now with chains attached ready for lifting. He covers up her head and moves over to the rope to start hauling it up onto its rail. The body rises up and the image is one similar to da Vinci's "Anatomical Man."

A buffer hits the end of the grill to start the body moving along the rail.

We see the body on the grill traveling along its rail, sparking as it moves and swinging violently to align itself to the sarcophagus.

Then Victor pulls on the chain to lower it to the sarcophagus below. He pulls the shroud from the body just before it is immersed into the sarcophagus.

He pumps the bellows with his foot and, as the fire starts to burn high, pulls the sarcophagus over it.

He pulls the needles from their racks. The sarcophagus moves into position under the eel sack. He rams the first needle home. More needles are inserted through the side of the sarcophagus and into the body.

Victor locks down the lid of the sarcophagus. He pulls the glass tube into its keepers, madly grabs the connectors at the main power point, and clips them onto the terminals. Sparks fly as they touch.

Power surges through the cylinders and along the copper wires.

The current flies around the attic room, along the wires and batteries and machines, and we follow Victor as he rushes round, checking his apparatus. He stands on top of the sarcophagus as he releases the eels into it.

VICTOR

Live!!!!

We hear Victor yelling from the attic, and—

Cut to:

MANSION GRAND STAIRCASE
Night

Henry, bathed in sweat, unkempt, hands shaking, is close to a nervous breakdown.

HENRY (screaming)

No!!

MANSION ATTIC
Night

Outside the mansion, we see light coming from the cupola as it is lit up by the lightning.

Inside, we move from the cupola to see Victor lift the lid off the tank and bend down to tie it off.

He stands back up and looks down into the steaming liquid. Then reaches into the fluid. He pulls out his creation, cradling the head and neck as one would cradle a newborn infant's…

Massive suture marks bisect her neck and collarbone where pieces were joined. He bangs her on the back and strokes her head.

A whisper:

VICTOR
Live.

Her mouth is gaping to draw air but finding fluid in the lungs. He clutches her tight, pounding her back to start her breathing, as her lungs heave violently to dispel the fluid.

He starts to lift her out of the sarcophagus. He wipes off the muck, cleansing her face as she shivers and coughs.

He dresses her in her wedding dress, forces the wedding ring on her finger.

Elizabeth sits on a box, her head drooping, as Victor stands in front of her.

VICTOR
Say my name. Say my name.

She is blank. Dazed. Stunned. Not a flicker of recognition.

Victor kneels at her feet.

VICTOR (continued)
Say my name. Please, you must remember. Elizabeth…Elizabeth.

She lifts her head to look at him. A flicker in her eyes? His saying "Elizabeth" seems to have triggered some memory.

Now we see that she is a hideous amalgam of Elizabeth's head and face, and Justine's torso.

VICTOR
That's it, you remember. It's all right…

Slowly she reaches to touch his face. Victor starts to help her to her feet.

VICTOR (continued)
Stand…Stand. Yes, yes, come on, come on.

Victor slowly helps her to her feet. And slowly…ever so slowly…she raises her bony white hand before her eyes…staring at it…trying to puzzle out its meaning…perhaps the vaguest shred of recognition…and the hand continues to rise…creeping slowly toward his shoulder…and coming to rest there. We see the wedding ring on her finger. He smiles.

She starts to raise her other hand and Victor takes it as if ready to dance.

VICTOR
You remember, you remember…

At first it's imperceptible…just the slightest motion, and then it grows into the vaguest sway…tears are glistening in Victor's eyes as she begins to move. Lurching. Faltering. Unsure.

Trace memories. A waltz.

VICTOR
That's it, that's it, that's it, that's it.

And here we are treated to the most sweepingly romantic and hair-raisingly demented image of the film: Victor dances with his dead bride, showing her the way, begging her to remember, please remember, and now the "Waltz/Love Theme" really comes back to haunt us as the music swells, incred-

ibly lush and deranged, dissonant and echoing through Victor's head, music only he can hear…

And the worst part? The very worst thing of all? There on the shelf. A large formaldehyde jar. Justine's severed head. Watching them through the glass with dead, sightless eyes. Watching them dance. Still a wallflower? No. She's finally finishing her dance with Victor…most of her, anyway. Under the circumstances, it'll have to do.

And the waltz goes on, madder and madder, sweeping in glorious circles. Elizabeth drops her head back and they dance on, Elizabeth laughing. Victor picks her up and sweeps her around the room, joining in with her laughter.

Intercut with this action are happy, beautiful images of Victor and Elizabeth dancing in the past.

The insane music swells louder and louder, higher and higher, reaching toward its crescendo with jagged glass claws…

…and it all screeches to a stop as Victor turns to see the Creature standing by the sarcophagus,

silhouetted in the lightning…

    Music echoes abruptly away into silence. Nothing now but rain and distant thunder.

CREATURE

She's beautiful.

VICTOR

She's not for you.

CREATURE (*to Elizabeth*)

Come.

The Creature raises his hand, beckoning…She is drawn to him.

VICTOR

Elizabeth?…say my name…

She takes a faltering step towards the Creature.

CREATURE

Elizabeth, yes.

VICTOR (*shouts*)

Elizabeth!

She turns to Victor.

CREATURE

You're beautiful.

She turns back to the Creature.

VICTOR (*desperate*)

Say my name.

She looks back at Victor.

CREATURE

Come to me.

She walks up to the Creature and gazes into his eyes, studying his face. Her fingertips trace his massively scarred flesh. A beat. A frown. A puzzlement. This isn't right. People don't look like this. They're not stitched together out of pieces of flesh like a patchwork.

    She looks at her hands. Dead and white. One not even hers—it belonged to Justine. Suture scars mar the other wrist. She looks down at herself: the body that isn't hers either. Realization and horror creep into her eyes, and she turns to Victor: Why do I look like this? What's happened to me? Oh, God, what's happened to me?

She tries to speak.

VICTOR

Say my name.

ELIZABETH

Vic–tor…

VICTOR

That's right, Elizabeth.

ELIZABETH

Vic–tor.

The Creature grabs her and turns her to face him and starts to dance with her, turning her round and round.

CREATURE

No…She's mine!

Victor can stand it no longer. He rushes forward to try to grab her from the Creature. They tussle for her, Victor trying to prise away the Creature's arm.

VICTOR

No, leave her alone!

CREATURE (*continued*)

Get away from her! She's mine!

VICTOR

She's mine! She said my name! She remembers!

Yes. She remembers. Not much, but enough. She shrieks out and struggles free of them.

ELIZABETH

No…!

Shrieking as she sails across the room. She turns to Victor, running her hands over her scarred hand and face…

    …and heads straight for the kerosene lamp, snatching it up before they can stop her.

VICTOR (*continued*)

No!

She spins to face them, holding them breathlessly at bay with the threat of the lamp, twitching from one to the other. But it's not just the lamp, it's the look of sheer loathing in her eyes. Loathing for them for what they've done to her—loathing for herself for what she's become.

    It turns out that the lady does know her own

mind. She wants no part of it—or them. Decision made. She crushes the lamp in her bare hands, drenching herself in a cascade of kerosene, and goes· up in a ball of flame.

She moves off down the stairs. Victor follows, then the Creature.

MANSION HALLWAY AND STAIRCASE
Night

A scream and the door explodes. Elizabeth hurtles shrieking toward the camera, still trying to claw the dead flesh away, pulling off giant flaming pieces of herself as she careens out the door and down the steps towards us,

Victor racing after her. The Creature follows them to the foot of the attic stairs and stops.

She sails down the hallway, setting fire to every-thing she passes, as she spins, screaming for the final torment to end. She hurls herself over the edge…and plummets to the floor far below. A pillar of flame leaps up on impact.

Cut to: Exterior shot of mansion burning.

BURNT-OUT MANSION
Day

Outside the remains of the burnt-out mansion Victor and Henry sit and talk. Begin on closeup of Victor's hands, fingers intertwined, and pan up to his gloomy face.

VICTOR
All that I once loved now lies in a shallow grave by my hand.

HENRY
(completely exhausted and verging on breakdown)
What will you do now?

VICTOR
Find him.

HENRY
You can't, Victor. Leave it. There's nothing else you
can do.

VICTOR
I can't, Henry, neither can he. We're both damned.
I know where he is going.

HENRY
Where?

VICTOR
To the world he would have lived in had I kept my
promise. The farthest reaches of the North Pole.

HENRY
Victor, if he doesn't kill you, the Arctic will.

VICTOR
Then at least something good will come of it.
(he turns to Henry)
You should have been my father's son; he would
have been so proud. God bless you, Henry.

HENRY
God forgive you, Victor.

VICTOR
Goodbye.

Victor stands and walks away.

134

When I quitted Geneva, my first labour was to gain some clue by which I might trace the steps of my fiendish enemy. But my plan was unsettled; and I wandered many hours around the confines of the town, uncertain what path I should pursue. As night approached, I found myself at the entrance of the cemetery where William, Elizabeth, and my father reposed. I entered it and approached the tomb which marked their graves....

The deep grief which this scene had at first excited quickly gave way to rage and despair. They were dead and I lived; their murderer also lived, and to destroy him I must drag out my weary existence. I knelt on the grass and kissed the earth, and with quivering lips exclaimed, "By the sacred earth on which I kneel, by the shades that wander near me...I swear to pursue the daemon, who caused this misery, until he or I shall perish in mortal conflict....Let the cursed and hellish monster drink deep of agony; let him feel the despair that now torments me."...

I was answered through the stillness of night by a loud and fiendish laugh. It rung on my ears long and heavily; the mountains re-echoed it, and I felt as if all hell surrounded me with mockery and laughter....I darted toward the spot from which the sound proceeded; but the devil eluded my grasp. Suddenly the broad disk of the moon arose, and shone full upon his ghastly and distorted shape, as he fled with more than mortal speed.

I pursued him; and for many months this has been my task....Amidst the wilds of Tartary and Russia, although he evaded me, I have ever followed in his track....[S]ometimes he himself, who feared that if I lost all trace I should despair and die, often left some mark to guide me. The snows descended on my head, and I saw the print of his huge step on the white plain....Sometimes, indeed, he left marks in writing on the barks of the trees, or cut in stone, that guided me, and instigated my fury....

As I still pursued my journey to the northward, the snows thickened, and the cold increased to a degree almost too severe to support....The triumph of my enemy increased with the difficulty of my labours. One inscription that he left was in these words: "Prepare! your toils only begin: wrap yourself in furs, and provide food, for we shall soon enter upon a journey where your sufferings will satisfy my everlasting hatred."

Cut to: Establishing shot of the *Alexander Nevsky* locked in the snow, and then to:

WALTON'S CABIN ON THE *NEVSKY*
Twilight

Closeup on Victor's tired face.

VICTOR

I followed the trail he left for me. North, always North. For months now, with one intent—to kill him. And now I'm tired. *(he closes his eyes)* I'm so very, very tired.

Victor drifts off to sleep. Walton places his hand on Victor's brow.

NEVSKY DECK
Twilight

Walton emerges on deck, armed with his gun, to face Grigori and the mutinous crew. They wait for some news from Walton, quieting as he appears.

GRIGORI

What did he say?

WALTON

He's dead. He died raving about some phantom.

GRIGORI *(anxious)*

What is out there, Captain?

WALTON

He told me a story that…It couldn't be true. He was mad…I think.

A light breeze can be heard in the rigging.

WALTON *(continued)*

A warming breeze. The ice will melt yet.

GRIGORI

And what then, Captain?

WALTON

We head north.

A moment of icy tension. An exchange of looks. Brief shot of the furious, mutinous crew.

GRIGORI *(firmly)*

No.

Suddenly we hear the noise of a flapping door from behind. Walton leads some of the men in the direction of the noise.

WALTON'S CABIN
Twilight

In the corridor outside the cabin, Walton silences the pursuing crew with a gesture.

WALTON

Wait. Listen.

I entered the cabin, where lay the remains of my ill-fated and admirable friend. Over him hung a form which I cannot find words to describe; gigantic in stature, yet uncouth and distorted in its proportions. As he hung over the coffin, his face was concealed by long locks of ragged hair; but one vast hand was extended, in colour and apparent texture like that of a mummy. When he heard the sound of my approach, he ceased to utter exclamations of brief and horror, and sprung towards the window. Never did I behold a vision so horrible as his face, or such loathsome, yet appalling hideousness. I shut my eyes involuntarily, and endeavoured to recollect what were my duties with regard to this destroyer. I called on him to stay.

[letter from Captain Walton to his sister]

They freeze at the sound of soft weeping.

Walton and the crew members enter the cabin and ease forward to get a closer look at the bed. Victor is lying on it, eyes closed, dead. A dark figure sits hunched and weeping at the bedside, holding Victor's journal. Walton and the crew are stunned.

WALTON

Who are you?

The figure looks up, revealing its face in the dim light.

CREATURE

He never gave me a name.

The crew are startled but intrigued. They train their guns on the Creature, who remains unconcerned.

WALTON

Why do you weep?

CREATURE

He was my father.

Walton is moved.

ICE FLOE
Twilight

The crew of the *Nevsky* are on the ice. The body of Victor lies on an impressive bier of wood, stacked and lashed. His body is wrapped in rough canvas, his face as dead and white as the ice.

Walton and crew stand facing the bier as Walton reads a passage from the Bible. A little way off on the ice, the Creature stands weeping.

WALTON
"And yea, I gave my heart to know wisdom
and to know madness and folly:
and I perceived that all is vanity
and vexation of spirit.

"For in much wisdom is much grief:
and he that increaseth knowledge,
increaseth sorrow.

"For God shall bring every work and every secret thing into judgment whether it be good, or whether it be evil."

Walton glances at Grigori and nods. Three men run forward and begin dousing the pyre with lamp oil, soaking it.

Walton takes the torch from Grigori and moves over to a flambeau to light it. . .

The Creature, still weeping, walks slowly towards the bier.

GRIGORI

Captain. . . ?

WALTON

He has the right to bear witness.

Suddenly the ice beneath them begins to shake.

Within seconds there is an explosion of water and ice behind them. It goes with terrifying speed and force: *Crack!* Another eruption. *Crack!* And another. *Crack!* Ice cascading skyward.

OLD SAILOR *(Tommy)*

Jesus, it's breakin' up!

The ice between the Creature and Victor explodes, sending the Creature flying. He lands in the water. Most of the crew are in full retreat, scrambling for their lives. Ice is detonating for miles around as if pounded by artillery.

WALTON

Back to the ship!!!

Crack! The ice in front of Walton erupts, sending him back. The torch goes flying as Walton is thrown backwards.

The torch lands on the ice in front of Walton. He reaches for it, but it is pulled from his reach and moves away from them on an iceberg. Grigori scrambles up beside Walton.

GRIGORI

Leave the damn torch! Leave it!

Walton and Grigori turn to see: the Creature appear from under the surface of the water. He sees the torch floating away and swims towards it.

Walton and Grigori: a look.

The Creature reaches the iceberg where the torch lies. He looks grimly back to Walton, who beckons to him: Come. Grab my hand.

WALTON

Come with us.

CREATURE *(slowly)*

I am done with Man.

He takes hold of the torch and then swims on towards the ever-revolving bier.

Walton and Grigori slog grimly on across the disintegrating ice. They leap a huge gap between the tipping icebergs. The crew running back towards the boat try to clamber up the side of the ship, clinging on for dear life.

Those already on board lean over the side, pulling the rest of the crew onto the deck. Several men plummet into the icy water as they tumble over the moving plates, slipping and sliding.

Grigori is hauled from the frigid Arctic ice and hoisted up the side of the ship. Then Walton jumps for the ship, missing his footing, but regains it and climbs up.

NEVSKY DECK
Twilight

Walton lurches to the gunwale, gazing off. The men crowd to his side.

Out on the ice floe, the Creature swims on, his head barely breaking the water, the torch held high to keep it burning. Relentlessly determined, gasping and sinking beneath the surface…This is the most grueling effort we've ever seen.

He pauses, exhausted—almost there—looks at the bier, considers, and swims on…and finally

grasps with frozen fingers the ice floe upon which lies Victor's funeral pyre.

He hauls himself from the water. Never giving up.

The Creature moves around to stand behind Victor's head on the bier, holding the torch aloft. Victor himself lies serenely, content to be shown the way…

The Creature turns his face to sky, gulping air, spreading his arms wide in sublime triumph. He glances at the torch burning low in his outstretched hand, the pitch almost gone, sputtering and trailing smoke.

He looks down at Victor. The oil-soaked canvas.

Walton and the crew gaze in horror, realization dawning:

The Creature turns his gaze one last time toward Heaven. Finding in these last moments the sympathy he'd so long sought.

He rams the torch into the pyre beneath him. White-hot ignition. Ultimate redemption. *Whump!* A massive ring of flame engulfs the bier, pushing a huge fiery fist into the sky, blossoming, roiling.

Walton and the crew gaze on in wonder and horror as they watch the Creature, now cradling Victor in his arms. We glimpse the faces through the flames. Father and son. Close at last. Peace at last. The Creature does not flinch.

Walton stands at the gunwale, the crew at his side, watching the pyre burn far off. The aurora borealis dances mysteriously on the horizon. Distant slivers of lightning kiss the world.

GRIGORI *(grim)*

Where to now, Captain?

WALTON *(softly)*

Home.

ARCTIC ICE
Twilight

Image of the flaming pyre is intercut with the ship moving off in full sail.

The pyre, bearing the Modern Prometheus and his son, disappears into the mist, borne away by the waves and lost in darkness and distance.

THE END

TriStar Pictures *Presents*

In association with Japan Satellite Broadcasting, Inc.
and The IndieProd Company

An American Zoetrope Production

A Kenneth Branagh *Film*

Robert De Niro

Kenneth Branagh

MARY SHELLEY'S
FRANKENSTEIN

Tom Hulce

Helena Bonham Carter

Aidan Quinn

Ian Holm

John Cleese

Music by Patrick Doyle

Costumes designed by James Acheson

Editor Andrew Marcus

Production Designer Tim Harvey

Director of Photography Roger Pratt, B.S.C.

Co-Producers Kenneth Branagh *and* David Parfitt

Executive Producer Fred Fuchs

Screenplay by Steph Lady *and* Frank Darabont

Produced by Francis Ford Coppola, James V. Hart, John Veitch

Directed by Kenneth Branagh

The Filmmakers
and Their Creations

"It was indeed a filthy process in which I was engaged...."

—*Mary Shelley*

Reanimating a classic story on screen is among filmmaking's greatest challenges, the more so when an earlier movie of the same story—the 1931 *Frankenstein* with Boris Karloff's immortal performance as the Creature—was a cinematic landmark. But it was a challenge that the makers of *Mary Shelley's Frankenstein* relished.

Fittingly, it was a team of English and American film artists that gave birth to the project. Universal's 1931 *Frankenstein* was a Hollywood adaptation of the British writer's novel, directed by Englishman James Whale. This film began when screenwriter

Steph Lady's draft *Frankenstein* screenplay caught the interest of James V. Hart, who had scripted another recent retelling of an epic horror tale: *Bram Stoker's Dracula*. Hart brought it to Francis Ford Coppola and Fred Fuchs at American Zoetrope, who at the time were immersed in making *Dracula*.

Coppola immediately recognized that the time was right for a new rendition of Mary Shelley's story. We live, after all, in an age of discovery not unlike the one she depicted in *Frankenstein*—an age where replacement body parts are commonplace fact, and the idea of genetically cloning a human being is discussed not as fantasy but as a scientific possibility. Coppola says of *Frankenstein:*

> "I had always loved the novel and had thought of remaking it long before I did *Dracula.* I've always been interested in the classics, particularly in the horror zone, and I'm especially interested in going back to the original source material."

The premise from the start was to make a film that was truer to Mary Shelley, both in letter and spirit, than any preceding version, but that also spoke , directly to today's audiences.

TriStar Pictures soon added its considerable weight as the parent studio. Production executives Marc Platt, Stacey Snider, Michael Besman, and John Levy joined with Coppola, Fuchs, and Hart to develop the project, retaining Lady for further drafts and then bringing in the more seasoned Frank Darabont, a great fan of the Shelley novel. The producers were also pursuing their two main targets:

first, to find a director whose enthusiasm and talents were up to the job (Coppola himself chose not to take on another big directing assignment on the heels of *Dracula*); and equally important, to land Robert De Niro for the role of the Creature.

Directing and Starring in…

Kenneth Branagh was just completing post-production work on his superb interpretation of Shakespeare's *Much Ado About Nothing* when Coppola contacted him about the possibility of directing *Mary Shelley's Frankenstein*. It would be a production of much greater scope than any of the four pictures he had directed in his young career—but his ability to infuse classic literature with a contemporary sensibility had already been proven beyond doubt. Branagh says:

> "For me, this is less of a horror film and more of a larger-than-life gothic fairy tale. It's full of psy-

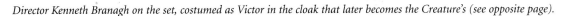

Director Kenneth Branagh on the set, costumed as Victor in the cloak that later becomes the Creature's (see opposite page).

Branagh checks a shot in his portable monitor.

you had the power to bring them back to life?"

As Branagh thought his way into the story, discovering more and more of its unexplored dimensions, it became clear to him that certain themes needed to come out in the screenplay. One key element to emerge was the relationship between Victor Frankenstein and his adopted sister Elizabeth, who becomes his soulmate and bride.

> "It was important to me to have a very strong woman's role in a film of this size, and not just a token love interest. All too often women are just the peripheral elements of the picture, and I wanted Elizabeth and Victor to be two equal partners, utterly entwined from the beginning. These two people were absolutely meant to be together."

Branagh takes the protagonist part of Victor Frankenstein as well as directing—the fifth feature film in which he has played this demanding double role. In 1988, his courageous and confident adaptation of Shakespeare's *Henry V* won lavish critical praise and many awards, including an Oscar for Best Costumes and Oscar nominations for Best Director and Best Actor.

For his next project, 1991's *Dead Again,* Branagh and his wife and co-star Emma Thompson moved to Hollywood, with Branagh not only directing but playing dual lead roles in this mystery of a love that survives death and the passage of time—a theme he returns to in *Frankenstein.*

Next came the modestly budgeted *Peter's Friends,* a contemporary comedy/drama in which Branagh collaborated with a sparkling ensemble of British and American comic actors, including Stephen Fry, Hugh Laurie, and Rita Rudner. In the same year, 1992, Branagh directed Sir John Gielgud and Richard Briers (Grandfather in *Mary Shelley's Frankenstein*) in the short film *Swan Song,* nominated for an Oscar. And before the year was out, he had also co-produced, directed, and starred in *Much Ado About Nothing.* With its bold casting (Denzel Washington, Keanu Reeves, and Michael Keaton among others) and dynamic pacing, this film did more to revive interest in Shakespeare among the general public than any dozen theater festivals.

chological insights about family. It deals with the themes of parenting and responsibility, of birth and death, of man's arrogance in the face of nature and his inhumanity to man. The image I kept seeing was of a child in the delivery room, delivered and then abandoned, squealing and screeching. That is essentially what happens in the book. Frankenstein abandons the child and thereafter suffers the appalling consequences of his actions.

"I knew that many films based on the story had been made, and so I also knew that the story must have a very strong hold on people. When I read the novel, I was very forcibly reminded about why that should be. The idea of a man playing God and cheating death is a primal myth and poses several questions: is it evil for a man to disregard the consequences of bringing another creature into the world? Who is more evil—Frankenstein or his abandoned Creature? What would you do if someone you loved died, and

Branagh and cameraman set up a dolly shot on the Ingolstadt set.

Francis Coppola, whose production role in *Mary Shelley's Frankenstein* included casting assistance and on-set consultation during rehearsals and early phases of photography, discovered a kindred spirit in Branagh: "He's clearly an energetic young man—I recognized in him some of the same kind of energy and competence to do whatever it takes that I fancied I had myself, also coming out of the theater. I was very impressed with Kenneth's overall approach and control; the production has been flawlessly executed." For his part, Branagh was appreciative of the older filmmaker's "supportive and inspiring presence" on the set and behind the scenes, saying, "I'm grateful for the opportunity to have a genius looking over my shoulder."

Branagh, with his longtime collaborator David Parfitt and David Barron, assembled the production team for the film at Shepperton Studios, under the rubric of Shelley Films, Ltd. Among them were many of the most creative figures in Britain's film community, and many had worked with Branagh on previous productions, lending a sense of cohesiveness and a "family" atmosphere to the shoot.

The only American producer on the team was the highly respected John Veitch, engaged by TriStar to move to London to oversee the production, whose huge scope and big budget would be a new experience for Branagh's mainly English team. Veitch, who had been involved in the production of more than 500 films in Hollywood, including numerous classics during his time as head of Columbia Pictures, had recently served as co-producer on *Bram Stoker's Dracula*. He recalls: "Ken agreed to do the picture providing it was done in England, including post-production. Though many pictures were being made there, they were not of this scope. So we were fortunate to get the top talent available at that time."

Principal photography took place mainly at London's Shepperton Studios, over a 16-week period

The child actors in character: left to right, Rory Jennings Linnane as Young Victor, Christine Cuttall as Young Justine, and Hannah Taylor-Gordon as Young Elizabeth.

from October 1993 to February 1994 with another week of location shooting in the Swiss Alps.

The Players

To those familiar only with old film versions of the Frankenstein story, just one character really stands out: the haplessly destructive being known as "the Monster" or "the Creature," incarnated by Boris Karloff and generally played within that mold.

In dramatizing *Mary Shelley's Frankenstein*, then, Kenneth Branagh and his colleagues faced two daunting challenges: finding a performer and a performance strong enough to equal that cinematic icon, and making sure that the other characters in Shelley's richly populated novel were given sufficient scope and substance. They wanted to move as far as possible from the comic-book treatment of the story and its characters: a big dumb monster, a mad sci-

entist, and some oddball supporting caricatures.

Says Casting Director Priscilla Johns, "Every one of the characters has a definite life." From the leads and major supporting roles down to the children who play younger versions of Victor, Elizabeth, and Justine, much care was devoted to finding actors who could create realistic portrayals and relationships within a story founded on a fantasy. The result, reflected in the acting and the production design, was a kind of "heightened realism" in which people and places seem natural but a bit larger than life.

Another important consideration—one of which Branagh is always conscious—was that the story not become mired in period detail. Says Johns:

"You have to be awfully careful that you don't start thinking in terms of making a costume drama. You're making a story that happens to be set in 1794, but the characters must be as real to

Robert De Niro as Frankenstein's Creature.

us now. And if you put any barriers up—costume, period airs and graces, whatever—then people will not identify with those characters and their problems, which are pretty well the same as we're having to deal with today.

"So when casting actors, you must get a truthfulness—with all due respect, not a Shakespearean stage performance of the conventional kind, where people switch off because the dialogue and costumes don't make it real for them. But with an approach like Ken used in *Much Ado*, suddenly it all makes sense. They're using the same language; they're just delivering it differently. So that's what we were looking for: an accurate way of delivering our perception of what it was like then.

"The actors had to be extremely free and very real. And the performances had to be strong—

149

not over-the-top, but strong enough not to be swallowed up by the magnficent sets."

The Creature/Robert De Niro

Often a brilliant stroke of casting can ignite a spark that makes a film project catch fire. Certainly, as Kenneth Branagh observes, many people will want to see Robert De Niro's interpretation of Frankenstein's Creature, as they would wish to see a great stage actor's Hamlet or Othello. And the famed actor brought to this role the kind of meticulous preparation and attention to detail for which he has long been noted.

The script called for a very different kind of Creature than we have seen on screen before. Kenneth Branagh notes:

"He had to be hideous, but he also had to be terribly sympathetic because of his terrible plight. He has been hurriedly thrown together and thrown into life, and then abandoned. I wanted a wise and intelligent and multifaceted Creature who could be angry and even funny at times, and who would have a sense of humor, however darkly ironic. It became obvious that we had to cast an actor who could have great compassion and wit and strength and violence and danger about him. Few combine these extraordinary things as well as Robert De Niro."

It was this approach to the character that led the actor to accept the role. Not for De Niro the lumbering, inarticulate monsters of previous films. His

De Niro in full make-up confers with Branagh during a break in shooting.

Creature is an infinitely complex thing: gruesome but sensitive, murderous but childlike, chilling but also sympathetic. De Niro says:

"I decided that the way Ken was going to make it different from previous versions, to give it a deeper meaning than just another horror film, was good. I liked the script and I was confident that it would be interesting. A good part that complements the story, and vice versa…a good character that has some depth to it…they're hard to come by."

De Niro came to *Mary Shelley's Frankenstein* from directing and starring in his own film *A Bronx Tale*. "I wanted to direct," he says with relish, "because I wanted to stand back and watch while the actor doing the scene is freezing half-naked in the middle of winter. Meanwhile the director is all bundled up, watching the seventh take."

These comments may have haunted the actor during the filming of *Mary Shelley's Frankenstein*, where he had to meet extraordinary physical demands. His full-body prosthetic make-up took many laborious hours to apply—up to ten on some days, followed by another six or seven hours of shooting. And his tasks in front of the camera included swimming in Arctic-temperature waters and leaping on and off a cart of plague-ridden "corpses."

Yet, according to Kenneth Branagh, his attention never flagged: "He's the most focused actor I've ever come across. He would come to the set having done all his work and all his worrying in advance, and would enjoy the work. He would do what I asked and put himself into my hands. As a director there is nothing better you can ask for. When a supremely talented actor does that, I consider it one of the best working relationships I've ever had."

De Niro has worked with most of the leading directors in contemporary cinema, including Elia Kazan, Martin Scorsese, Francis Ford Coppola, Brian De Palma, Bernardo Bertolucci, Roland Joffé, and Sergio Leone. His own recent experience as actor/director heightened his appreciation for Branagh's ability to shift gears smoothly: "Ken had a big job directing the film and a bigger acting part than I had in *A Bronx Tale*. But I never felt uncomfortable about his attention to all the performances. He understands how actors work and how they talk."

De Niro's extraordinary career has been distinguished by, among other things, his long and fruitful partnership with Martin Scorsese. Together they have made seven films, including the classics *Mean Streets, Taxi Driver*, and *Raging Bull*. His portrayal of the young Vito Corleone in Coppola's *The Godfather, Part II* won him an Academy Award for Best Supporting Actor in 1974, and he was subsequently nominated for his work in *Taxi Driver, The Deer Hunter*, Penny Marshall's *Awakenings*, and *Cape Fear*. Other films in which he has given memorable performances include *Bang the Drum Slowly, The Last Tycoon, The Mission, Midnight Run*, and *Once Upon a Time in America*.

In 1988 De Niro co-founded the Tribeca Film Center in downtown New York, where his production company, also named Tribeca, develops new film and television projects. The center's state-of-the-art facilities are used by numerous other industry professionals as well.

The role of Victor Frankenstein is among Branagh's most complex and challenging to date.

Victor Frankenstein/Kenneth Branagh

Born in Belfast and raised in England, Branagh studied at the Royal Academy of Dramatic Art, and with the Royal Shakespeare Company in 1984, his roles included Henry V, the King of Navarre in *Love's Labors Lost*, and Laertes in *Hamlet*. In 1987 he formed his own Renaissance Theatre Company with actor David Parfitt, later to become Branagh's co-producer on several projects including *Mary Shelley's Frankenstein*. With Renaissance, he produced and appeared in several successful London and touring productions, as well as acting in numerous British television productions (including the BBC hit series "Fortunes of War," based on the *Balkan Trilogy* by Olivia Manning).

His most recent appearance on the stage was in a record-breaking RSC production of *Hamlet* in London and Stratford-on-Avon. In 1993 he was awarded the prestigious Michael Balcon Award by BAFTA for Outstanding Contribution to the Cinema, and became a member of the Board of Governors of the British Film Institute.

Branagh discusses his views on Victor's character in his Introduction to this book, and adds:

"Victor believes that God has done many amazing things, but that he can be improved upon. He feels the most terrible anguish when he loses his mother, from which he never fully recovers, and his efforts to create life are an attempt to ensure that he never loses anyone again. I think he is a man whose intentions are good, so the audience is able to understand him.

"This is a driven man, who is fired by his

work in a way that is alarming at times—something which, alas, I feel all too familiar with. Some would describe this large, lumbering film as a kind of monster I'm creating...."

To help keep his own performance on track amid the heavy demands of directing, Branagh called on production consultant Hugh Cruttwell, a former principal at RADA when Branagh was a student there. Since he began combining acting and directing, Branagh has asked Crutwell, now retired, to attend rehearsals and give notes on his performance in every film and play in which he has taken the dual role.

Elizabeth/Helena Bonham Carter

English actress Helena Bonham Carter has delivered a number of noteworthy performances in period roles since her first appearance in Trevor Nunn's *Lady Jane,* and she was at first reluctant to climb back into corsets and gowns for *Mary Shelley's Frankenstein.* But Kenneth Branagh convinced her that the role of Elizabeth, Victor's adopted sister and later his great love, would be no ordinary "love interest" but a true test of her maturity as an actress. She comments:

"Ken and I agreed on the need for Elizabeth to be Victor's equal and not just decorative. He wanted a lot of passion and guts which would make her a strong character, and the film really demanded it.

It has an epic, romantic sweep and an emotional fullbloodedness, which is very much reflected in Victor and Elizabeth's relationship. Through her love, Victor has the chance to redeem himself. The fact that he doesn't only serves to heighten the tragedy, because he has all the more to lose.

"The script touched me very much, in the way it deals with the themes of parenting and

have not always explored all her qualities as an actress: she has a terrific sense of fun, as well as intelligence and power. She contributed a great deal to the development of Elizabeth's role."

Bonham Carter made her international reputation with three film portrayals of E. M. Forster heroines, in *A Room with a View, Where Angels Fear to Tread,* and *Howards End,* and also appeared as Ophelia opposite Mel Gibson in Franco Zeffirelli's film of *Hamlet.* But other roles, notably as Marina Oswald in the TV film about Lee Harvey Oswald's wife, have demonstrated her flair for modern characterizations.

Henry/Tom Hulce

Tom Hulce is one of two American actors in the film who are more accustomed to playing leading roles, but who welcomed the chance to work in one of Kenneth Branagh's ensemble casts. Hulce provides some of the film's lighter moments, creating an engaging portrait of Victor's university friend Henry Clerval. An effective foil to the intense, obsessed Victor, Hulce's Henry takes a lighthearted attitude towards his studies, more motivated to become a doctor by the chance to meet rich ladies than by discovering the secret of life.

Hulce is best known for his tour de force performance as Mozart in Milos Forman's *Amadeus,* for which he received Academy Award and Golden Globe nominations, and won Italy's Donatello Award. He starred with Steve Martin in *Parenthood,*

loving, of birth and death. I knew Ken would make something wonderful of it, and I was very interested to work with an actor who was directing as well. It was a wonderfully collaborative experience."

Of his leading lady, Branagh says, "It was important to me to have a strong woman's role in a film of this size, and it's one of the elements of the picture I am most proud of. In the past, Helena's roles

Aidan Quinn, as the young Captain Walton, meets Victor Frankenstein when his ship is stranded in the Arctic ice.

and recently did a delightfully sleazy turn as an ambulance-chasing lawyer in Peter Weir's *Fearless*. Other film credits include *National Lampoon's Animal House* and *Black Rainbow*. He is equally adept in stage roles, having starred as Hamlet in Washington, D.C.'s Shakespeare Theatre and in a production of *The Sisters Rosensweig* in Seattle, and was nominated for a Tony for his leading performance in *A Few Good Men* on Broadway.

Hulce says of Henry: "He's like Victor's conscience. He starts out with a very buoyant outlook, but gradually gets ground down by the events of the story. I thought it would be fun to work with Ken and the people he had assembled. It's sometimes fun not to play the main role but to be the support, and I was able to write in some scenes for the character, which I enjoyed."

Walton/Aidan Quinn

Mary Shelley's Frankenstein begins and ends in the frozen Arctic, where Mary Shelley provides an alter ego and a sympathetic audience for Victor Frank-

enstein in the person of Captain Robert Walton, a young explorer played in the film by the talented, magnetic Aidan Quinn. Walton's single-minded and suicidal pursuit of a sea passage to the North Pole clearly echoes Victor's obsessive quest, so his presence, while fairly brief, is pivotal.

Quinn's was one of the most physically difficult parts in the production: first he is drenched in a huge storm that nearly wrecks his ship—a full-size reproduction built on one of Shepperton's largest sound stages—and the rest of his scenes take place in conditions cold enough to freeze the real ice used on the set. Psychologically, the challenge was to feel firmly connected with the film's main action while acting only in scenes that occur on its periphery.

None of this stood in the way of Quinn's motivations to do the film:

"Not only was the script a real page-turner, but all the characters were well-written and required real acting, which is one of my criteria for taking on a role. I thought it was a great story with an

155

exciting cast—I can't think of better actors to work with. I also want to have respect for my director, and after seeing Ken's *Much Ado About Nothing*, I very much wanted to work with him. So I didn't really consider the cold and wet…of course, I hadn't realized what an incredibly realistic ship they had built, and the totally convincing way they were able to toss it around in the storm."

Quinn first attracted international attention in the sleeper hit *Desperately Seeking Susan*, with Madonna and Rosanna Arquette. He played Robert De Niro's brother in *The Mission*, and won critical praise in *Playboys* and Barry Levinson's *Avalon*. Other film credits include *The Handmaid's Tale*, *At Play in the Fields of the Lord*, and *Benny and Joon*.

His theater work includes *A Streetcar Named Desire* and the title role in an award-winning *Hamlet* in Chicago. He also starred in Sam Shepard's *Fool for Love* at the Circle Theater.

Waldman/John Cleese

Surely Branagh's most intriguing casting decision for *Mary Shelley's Frankenstein* was tapping comic mastermind John Cleese to play the enigmatic Dr. Waldman, Victor's mentor at the university and his predecessor in experiments to reanimate the dead. Branagh explains the seeming paradox:

> "I didn't want Waldman to be the clichéd old mad scientist. I was looking for the terrific melancholy to which great comedians have access, because I think Waldman lives with guilt and dread about his secret past and that makes him very sad. There's a tremendous compassion, wisdom, and sadness in those great big John Cleese eyes."

Mindful of his indelible image as a comic performer, Cleese was determined to change his looks drastically to play Waldman. "Many people have said that they only have to see me smile," notes the

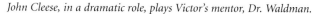

John Cleese, in a dramatic role, plays Victor's mentor, Dr. Waldman.

156

actor, "and Ken and I agreed that this would not exactly help the movie. I discovered ten years ago that changing my mouth is the best way of altering my appearance, so I had my dental mechanic make a prosthetic. And I wore a wig modeled on the hair of a scientist in a painting by Joseph Wright of Derby."

Cleese admits that he was not a fan of the Frankenstein story before reading this new version: "I'd only seen one earlier *Frankenstein,* and my father had to take me out of the cinema because I got scared. This must have been about 1946."

John Cleese's show business career began at Cambridge University, where he joined the famed Footlights comedy revue team that has launched so many careers. Following an appearance on Broadway with Footlights and several British TV shows on the cutting edge of comedy, Cleese and some friends in 1969 founded "Monty Python's Flying Circus"—eventually to become one of the most enduring phenomena in the entertainment world. Three "Python" feature films were made, and Cleese later created his own TV series, "Fawlty Towers."

His film appearances have included *Time Bandits, The Great Muppet Caper,* and, in a straight role, Lawrence Kasdan's *Silverado.* Cleese also played a dramatic role (Petruchio) in Jonathan Miller's BBC-TV production of *The Taming of the Shrew,* and he wrote as well as starred in the huge comedy hit of 1988 *A Fish Called Wanda* (which earned him an Academy Award nomination for Best Screenplay).

Although he admirably fulfills his mission of creating a wholly new persona on screen in this film, Cleese not surprisingly contributed much to the easygoing atmosphere on the set. "There was a particularly good feeling between the cast and crew, but I was still surprised how many times Ken, Tom Hulce, and I were laughing together only ten seconds before very serious takes," he recalls. Outtakes from the still photography, in fact, show Cleese supine on a primitive operating table, with a gaping, bloody "wound" in his stomach and a maniacal grin on his face.

And the Supporting Cast...

The remaining characters in *Mary Shelley's Frankenstein* are played by a cast of both veterans and newcomers, several of whom have worked with Kenneth Branagh in past productions.

Top: Cherie Lunghi. Above: Trevyn McDowell.

As the lovely but doomed Justine, the housekeeper's daughter who adores Victor in vain, young Trevyn McDowell came to the film from her starring role as Rosamund in the BBC's high-profile series *Middlemarch.* An innocent casualty of horrible circumstance, Justine is a victim not only of unrequited love but also of rough justice at the hands of a Geneva mob. She has suffered, too, from her mother's indifference and even hostility. Notes Mc-

Dowell, "She has no real confidence in herself, and finally I think she goes a little mad under the pressure of being falsely accused of murder." Raised in South Africa, McDowell has appeared in several popular British TV series, and on stage in various London productions.

Grandfather, the old blind man who tries to befriend the Creature after he takes refuge at a peasant family's hovel, is played by the prolific actor Richard Briers, best known for roles in British television comedies and in earlier Branagh films and stage productions. He played Malvolio in *Twelfth Night* on stage, Bardolph in *Henry V*, and Leonato in *Much Ado About Nothing* (the films), as well as starring with Sir John Gielgud in Branagh's Academy Award nominated short film *Swan Song*. Briers' theater work has included leading roles in the plays of Alan Ayckbourne and a recent West End revival of David Storey's *Home;* film credits include Michael Winner's *A Chorus of Disapproval*. In 1989 he was awarded an OBE for his services to the arts.

Another distinguished veteran, Ian Holm, portrays Victor's Father, a respected doctor whose family's tragic fate renders him a broken man. Hailed for his performances in every medium, Holm's film credits include the role of the coach in *Chariots of Fire* (an Academy Award–nominated performance), Ridley Scott's *Alien*, Zeffirelli's *Hamlet*, Branagh's *Henry V*, Terry Gilliam's *Brazil*, and David Cronenberg's *Naked Lunch*. A contract artist with the Royal Shakespeare Company for many years, his numerous stage roles range from Shakespeare to Pinter.

British actress Cherie Lunghi creates a winning portrait of Victor's beautiful and sweet-natured Mother, whose early death inspires his anguished determination to triumph over fate. Equally at home in Shakespeare or prime-time drama, Lunghi divides her successful career among the stage, film, and television. Her feature credits include John Boorman's *Excalibur* and Roland Joffé's *The Mission,* in which she appeared with two of this film's

The Frankenstein family at dinner: Ian Holm as Victor's Father in center.

Production Designer Tim Harvey and Construction Manager Michael Redding check a model of Victor's laboratory in the top of the mansion.

stars, Robert De Niro and Aidan Quinn—ironically, as De Niro's girlfriend who secretly loves his brother, played by Quinn. Lunghi has also appeared with Kenneth Branagh in a TV production of *The Lady's Not for Burning*.

Designing the Production

From the start, Kenneth Branagh had some definite ideas about what *Mary Shelley's Frankenstein* should look like:

> "I wanted to take a very familiar image and rework it, bring it up to date and make it fresh and exciting. It involves the sort of extremes that a gripping fairy tale might have: It's dark when it needs to be dark, and light and sunny when it needs to be. It's a film of many textures and many colors, and has an epic sweep to it because it's about building a creature that's larger than life. It's set in a countryside (the Swiss Alps) that's larger than life, and it takes two people on

a passionate, romantic, and ultimately tragic journey in which all the emotions are larger than life."

To realize this vision, Branagh and his co-producers made the decision at an early stage to shoot the film primarily in the studio rather than on location. They wanted as much control as possible of lighting effects, weather conditions, and sound. (A particular twist was the requirement to shoot several key scenes in an environment of snow and ice: the Arctic sequences at the start and finish, and the ice cave scene in the middle.) And one of the most critical production effects, the prosthetic make-up worn by Robert De Niro as the Creature, would be greatly facilitated by access to a fully equipped workshop and a large technical team.

Recalls co-producer David Parfitt: "Ken felt very strongly that we would lose control of the film if we used locations. He wanted a very particular larger-than-life but still realistic look, and the only

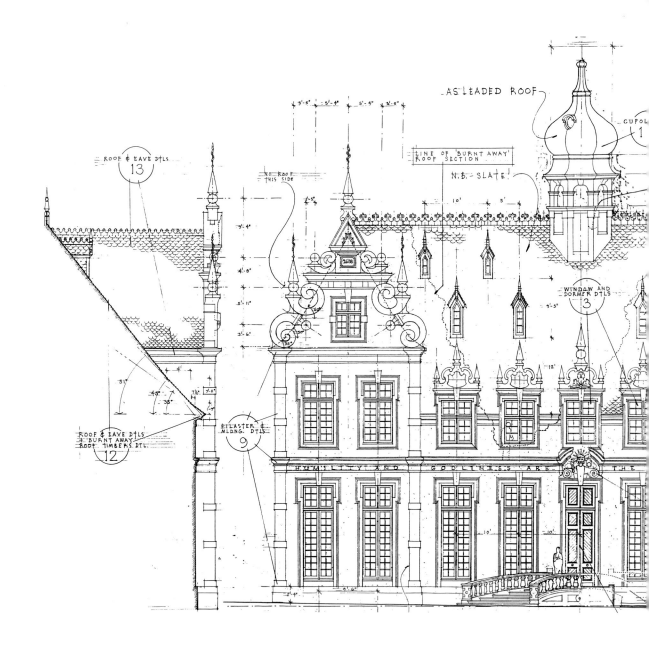

way to be sure of achieving consistency was to shoot most of it in a studio."

The British film industry was delighted when Branagh announced his choice for the filming as the Shepperton Studios outside London, where he had shot *Henry V.* The decision also gave Branagh access to many of Britain's leading creative figures in film, including several with whom he has had extensive working relationships.

Production Designer Tim Harvey and Art Director Martin Childs were key members of the team, having worked with Branagh on all his previous films. The resulting familiarity with each other's working methods made it easier to execute a production of the scope of *Mary Shelley's Frankenstein.* "It's an old-fashioned movie," says Harvey, "in the

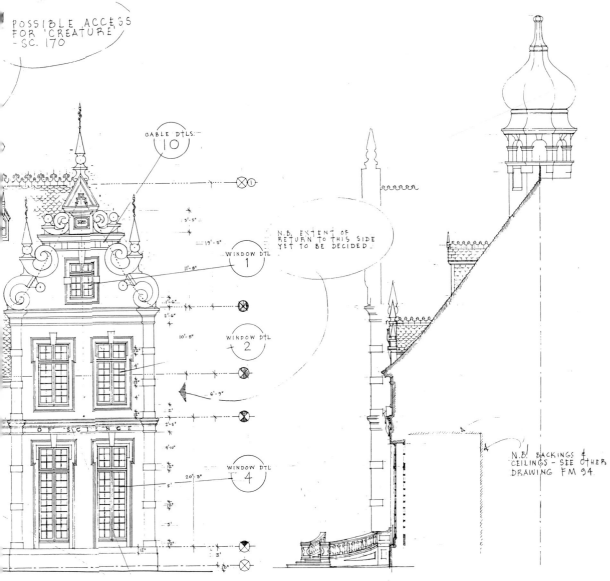

POSSIBLE ACCESS
FOR 'CREATURE'
- SC. 170

GABLE DTLS.
10

WINDOW DTL
1

N.B. EXTENT OF
RETURN TO THIS SIDE
YET TO BE DECIDED.

WINDOW DTL
2

WINDOW DTL
4

N.B. BACKINGS &
CEILINGS - SEE OTHER
DRAWING FM 34.

Part of a blueprint for the exterior of the Frankenstein mansion, and a color detail sketch of the ballroom.

sense that we had great expanses of builds and large crews—up to 200 people including construction at one time." Of the director and his development, Harvey notes, "He always knew exactly what he wanted…now he's more sure how to achieve it, in a way that makes him a little more demanding, but I don't mind that."

Shooting in the studio "you can concentrate your resources," Harvey points out. "In terms of time and effort, you can get much more return from your actors and control the pictures you get, rather than just allowing God to light it." Another reason to shoot on sound stages, Harvey explains, was "to achieve a sort of heightened realism that would be impossible to find in the real world." By heightened realism Branagh meant a larger-than-

life look in which certain details may be exaggerated for effect, while the audience still perceives the design as basically realistic.

"We went for scale rather than gothic detail," Harvey says. "We wanted contrasts in environment and people in a way that you get in gothic architecture, but without going for all the gothic details." Branagh also wanted to evoke the feeling of the period Shelley was writing about, without being overly committed to a specific "period" look. "It is not a documentary reproduction," Harvey emphasizes. "We chose the elements that suited our story, provided they did not actually jar."

Harvey and Childs have had ample experience at creating historical settings and emotional moods for Branagh's earlier productions—Tudor England

Opposite: Elizabeth's red costume is a spot of bright color in the realistically drab streets of Ingolstadt.
Above: The young Victor and Elizabeth meet in the vast ballroom.

and France for *Henry V,* 1930s Los Angeles for *Dead Again,* and romantic Tuscany for *Much Ado About Nothing.*

Still, the scale of *Mary Shelley's Frankenstein* dwarfed these earlier projects, calling for some of the most complex sets ever created in England. Seven sound stages were used. Five major and totally different sets were needed, along with a half dozen smaller interiors, all of which took about ten months of work before the start of principal photography. A week's location shooting in the Swiss Alps—which could never be adequately reproduced in the studio—rounded out the production.

The Frankenstein Mansion

Depicting the happy home where Victor spends his youth is one of the great contrasts this film makes with earlier Frankenstein movies and their gloomy, sinister castles. Here, bright primary colors were used to convey a mood of sunny warmth and festive elegance.

"The bright color was a very deliberate choice," says Tim Harvey. "We did not want a pallid, safe color range. We wanted it to come up and hit you in the eye rather than lie back in the landscape. At the same time, the sets don't shout out, 'Look at me, I'm different!' They are striking in wide shot but are not intended to dominate the scene in the closeups, which should have a naturalistic texture."

The result is seen most notably in the vast and airy ballroom of the mansion, with its exquisite wood-paneled walls washed in an intense blue. Built to an oversize scale, it is 128 feet long, and 64 feet wide, dominated at one end by a magnificent curved staircase that is a focal point for several of the film's most dramatic scenes. "If you really think about it," Harvey says, "there are no such rooms in real life, yet its effect on screen is realistic rather than stylistic."

The exterior of the mansion was likewise built

Above: Crowd scene outside the university gates. Opposite: The full-scale model of the Alexander Nevsky *during the storm sequence.*

oversize and painted a vivid ochre color for effect rather than strict realism. "Victor's home in reality would probably have been in soft greys; most of the buildings in Geneva and that area are," notes Harvey. "But it was more appropriate for us to go with strong color statements." Smaller set designs within the mansion were the upstairs corridor and bedrooms, and the attic where Victor assembles his second laboratory late in the story.

Ingolstadt and the University

A striking contrast to the cheerful mood of Victor's home is provided by the dark, grimy, disease-ridden town of Ingolstadt where he attends university and conducts his ill-fated experiments. For this massive set—the largest ever constructed at a British studio, even larger than *Batman's* Gotham City—the production appropriated the entire Shepperton back lot. At the center of the design is a vast cobbled market square with 50-foot city walls, surrounded by the imposing gates of the university, as well as

streets, alleys, Victor's boarding house, and other buildings of a German Swiss town in 1794.

The town encompassed a total area of 70,000 square feet, and over 57 miles of scaffolding were used. Its streets were laid with 2,630 square meters of cobbles, three boatloads worth imported from Portugal. Upwards of 50 technicians and carpenters labored for four months to build it. Notes Tim Harvey:

"We achieved a very strong graphic statement with large expanses of grim, decaying stone wall, punctuated by very small openings. It was true to Middle European walled cities but much exaggerated. The increased height gives a much more dramatic relationship of the people to the architecture, and gives the director the choice of dwarfing the characters to make them look relatively insignificant…or not. And the set decoration was meant to convey a strong sense of smell, perhaps of decay."

Top: The peasant hovel in winter "costume."
Above: Dr. Waldman's study.

Since it was an outdoor set, with shooting conducted from October to February, Ingolstadt had to survive the rigors of an English winter. It stood the test, and emerged all the more convincingly weathered.

A Ship on the Ice

An equally impressive feat of production design and execution was achieved on Shepperton's largest indoor sound stage: a three-masted eighteenth-century whaling vessel, which is thrashed by a violent storm and then frozen in the icy Arctic wastes. This is the *Alexander Nevsky*, a ship and its crew hired by the young Captain Walton to pursue his mad dream of discovering an open-sea passage to the North Pole, in the course of which he finds Victor Frankenstein in pursuit of the Creature.

Three ships actually were built: a full-sized vessel that measured 100 feet long and 23 feet wide, weighing 60 tons, as well as a quarter-sized replica and a 5-foot-long model. The smaller vessels were used to achieve perspective shots of the *Nevsky* across expanses of snow and ice. The life-sized ship could be moved around the stage only with airpads, normally used to float hovercraft. Fully rigged with immaculate attention to detail, it bore on its prow a figurehead in the likeness of Mary Shelley and holding a baby—an image suggesting the spirit of hope and endeavor in which the voyage and the film were made.

The snowscape in which the ship becomes locked was replicated with 23,000 cubic feet of polystyrene. For the final sequence when the ice breaks up, a million gallons of water were pumped into the stage, flooding it to the height of a man.

"Come Up to the Lab…"

A wealth of researched and imagined detail went into the building and furnishing of Victor's attic laboratory in Ingolstadt, where the climactic Creation sequence takes place. The array of equipment assembled by Victor includes reproductions of several devices used in the eighteenth and nineteenth centuries to generate electricity, as well as jars of assorted human parts in formaldehyde, and a system of tracks and pulleys to transport the Creature-in-progress around the lab.

The centerpiece is the "birthing" apparatus, consisting of a huge copper sarcophagus that functions as a "womb," which rests on a coal-fired furnace. Hanging from the rafters above looms a giant sack stitched together from skins. Jokingly referred to as the "bollock," or scrotum, it contains a mass of writhing and wriggling electric eels, released by Victor at the last moment to slither down a huge glass tube into the sarcophagus, providing the final

Original lab equipment used by Italian physician Luigi Galvani for his experiments in electrophysiology; used by the film's production team as models for Victor's equipment. The Bettmann Archive. Overleaf: Set of Victor's lodgings in Ingolstadt.

and decisive jolt of power to animate the Creature. Everywhere liquids bubble and wheels turn upon wheels. Tim Harvey says:

"Since Mary Shelley gives no details at all about how Frankenstein actually achieves the creation, we based our designs on what would have been possible for a scientist of that period to use in the way of equipment. We did a great deal of research on what was available, and the result was a very low-tech setup. Most of what Victor uses looks like it might have come from his landlady's kitchen.

"There are electric piles—jars with metals immersed in acids—which create a charge. We have steam engines driving a different form of generator, as well as something called a Wimshurst machine. All this apparent jumble of things was based on equipment that was in use at that time, or not long after, perhaps a few decades later than the period. We're not trying to make a documentary about the history of science; we've used what will most help the storytelling along. I hope some of our anachronisms do that, and don't leap out too strongly at the audience."

The Minor Sets

Considerable action in the film takes place in and around the peasant hovel outside Ingolstadt, where the Creatures takes refuge in a pigsty. This was one of the outdoor sets built at Shepperton, and the scenes where the Creature flees through the woods from pursuers were shot barely a hundred yards from the complex of studio offices and workshops.

Other notable interiors were Captain Walton's cabin on the *Nevsky,* where several dramatic scenes take place; a beautiful circular lecture hall at the Ingolstadt university; Dr. Waldman's study with its array of esoteric books, wall decoration, and scientific gear; and the bridal chamber at the lakeside lodge where Victor and Elizabeth's wedding night turns into a night of horror.

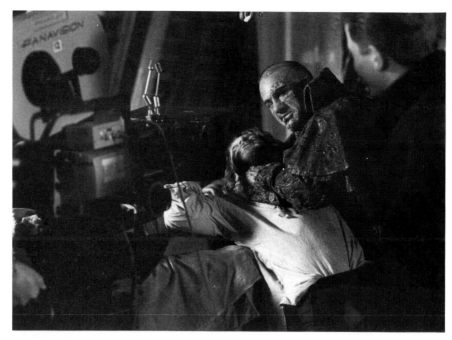

The camera moves in for a closeup on Victor and the Creature.

Sights and Sounds: The Cinematography and Score

Director of Photography Roger Pratt is a highly respected cameraman who can pick and choose his projects. His feature film credits over the last ten years include *Brazil* and *The Fisher King,* both for Terry Gilliam; Neil Jordan's *Mona Lisa;* Tim Burton's *Batman;* and most recently, Sir Richard Attenborough's *Shadowlands.*

Director Branagh describes the look and dynamic that the cinematography was meant to achieve:

> "We move the camera a great deal in this film. I wanted the audience to be on a roller coaster ride, to be swept viscerally along, to enter Victor's fevered imagination and get a rush of excitement to parallel the one coursing through his veins. Also it gives a sense of sweep and movement, of traveling a great deal. Lots of crane moves, especially in the creation sequences, each of which had to be very different."

Composer Patrick Doyle is another longtime collaborator of Kenneth Branagh's, having joined Branagh and Parfitt's Renaissance Theatre Company in 1987 as composer and musical director. A graduate of the Royal Scottish Academy of Music and Drama, he had previously pursued a double career as musician and actor.

He composed music for several of Renaissance's Shakespeare stage productions, and wrote his first film score for *Henry V;* its main theme won an award for Best Film Theme in 1989. He has since contributed the scores for all of Branagh's feature films excerpt *Peter's Friends,* which featured a collage of pop songs. He was nominated for a Golden Globe for his work in *Dead Again,* and the music for *Much Ado About Nothing* met with critical praise. Other credits include *Indochine, Into the West, Needful Things,* and *Carlito's Way.*

"Operatic" is one of the keywords used by Branagh to describe the film's tone, and Doyle agrees: "As soon as I read the script—when I was in tears on the plane—I knew that it would be a great big score. Ken's brief to me is always that the music should be instantly accessible and that it should be able to trigger an emotional response immediately."

Doyle's participation in the film went beyond the role of most composers, who generally don't come on the scene until well into post-production. "There are several dance sequences, and also a song," he explains, "so obviously those have to be written and staged in advance." He was on the set nearly throughout the shooting, teaching Richard Briers (Grandfather) to play the recorder, and working with Helena Bonham Carter on her piano playing. He also put his acting background to good use (as he has in other Branagh films), appearing on screen briefly as the conductor of the ballroom orchestra during the party scene—a classic case of art imitating life!

The Costumes

Academy Award winning costume designer James Acheson admits that he prefers doing period films. His two Oscars were for *The Last Emperor,* in which he re-created imperial and modern China, and for *Dangerous Liaisons,* set in eighteenth-century France. He says:

> "I enjoy doing the research for the period stories and discovering things that I don't know about, and I've always loved history. It was wonderful to go back to a period I had studied before (the eighteenth century) and look at it again. But Ken was not interested in historical accuracy for the sake of a purist re-creation. He wanted something more to do with colors, silhouettes, and texture—costumes that suggested the period rather than slavishly copied it. This is a sort of hybrid world…say, the middle to end of the eighteenth, edging into the nineteenth century."

For the costumers, the most demanding sequence was the ball at the Frankenstein mansion, for which more than 100 original costumes were needed. "We considered all sorts of different themes before we settled on a very classy, almost monochrome look for the gowns," Acheson says. "All were done in very pale colors. Ken had told me that he thought of the blue ballroom as a sort of heaven, so we thought of these pale costumes like clouds in the sky."

At the other end of the social and color spectrum, Acheson had to dress the peasant crowds in Ingolstadt, and even the rotting corpses of plague victims. "I wanted Ingolstatdt to look really Hogarthian in its filthiness," he says, "so I had people working full-time just on breaking down the

costumes and giving them real texture. Part of what I'm bringing to the picture, I hope, is to create people who don't look as if they'd just walked out of make-up, but as if they live and breathe and sleep and eat in what they've got on."

He also had the task of designing a single important garment for the Creature that would be worn nearly throughout the entire film:

> "I did about forty drawings of what this garment might do and how it might move, and eventually we settled on a big long coat. It starts out as a beautiful coat belonging to Victor Frankenstein, but from the moment the Creature puts in on and goes out into the rain, it belongs to him. From that moment, the coat starts to

Above: Two of the costumes for Victor and Elizabeth. Preceding page: One of James Acheson's early sketches for the Creature's single costume.

become more textured. It looks leathery, almost like the Creature's second skin, and as the story progresses it becomes filthier and increasingly torn and weathered."

The costumes of the loving couple, Elizabeth and Victor, are naturally more elaborate, and Acheson used them to suggest changes in mood and personality over the course of the film. Women's period costumes are a favorite of the designer's—"I'm mad about women in stays"—and Helena Bonham Carter declared that she'd never had such nice clothes to wear in a film. Acheson describes the transition the characters and costumes go through:

"You see her at the start, when she is Victor's young adopted sister, in pale blues and pinks. In the ball sequence she is in creams, those very pale colors. The transition starts when he goes away—she didn't want to be the simpering sister left behind and becomes quite assertive. When she goes to see him, she is in a very vivid, blood-red riding habit. It's as if the life blood has been

drained out of Victor at this point, and she is symbolically bringing her blood and her life force into his world.

"With Victor it's the opposite: there's a slight vanity about him, and his earlier costumes are quite chic and colorful, suggesting optimism. But in Ingolstadt, he has all the color drained out of him, as it were, into that laboratory. He comes back to Geneva drained, and dressed in grey."

A further challenge of dressing Branagh was the actor/director's desire to portray Victor in a more physical way than earlier films had done. He worked with a trainer and followed a diet and exercise regimen so that "the man completely changed shape," says Acheson. "The body we were putting clothes on at the start of rehearsals was completely different from the one we were dressing two months later. And he played a lot of those scenes in the laboratory stripped to the waist—he wanted to get quite away from the cliché of the wing-collared stock and maybe the apron with the sleeves rolled. His is a much more youthful, more energetic Frankenstein."

A make-up artist works on De Niro's prosthetic skin.

Essentially, though, this is not a film about costume. It's about strong, simple shapes rather than froth and furbelows. "I wanted to work on the film because I liked the script so much, and I really wanted to work with Kenneth Branagh," says Acheson. "I had turned down the invitation to work on *Henry V* and was glad of a second chance."

A New Creation—The Prosthetic Make-up

The image of Boris Karloff as Frankenstein's Monster in the 1931 movie classic is indelibly etched into

our visual memories. So the makers of *Mary Shelley's Frankenstein* felt it was critical to come up with an entirely original look for Robert De Niro's portrayal of the Creature. The task was entrusted to Special Effects Make-up Designer Daniel Parker, who worked in tandem with Chief Make-up Designer Paul Engelen. Parker and his company, Animated Extras, devised a total body prosthetic in which every inch of De Niro's body was covered with a new skin—a process that took between four and ten hours in the make-up chair and nine months of advance preparation.

Parker, whose credits include *Little Shop of Horrors*, *Robin Hood: Prince of Thieves*, and *The Crying Game*, tells the story of his team's remarkable achievement:

"Obviously we wanted to get right away from the Karloff make-up and look more closely at what Mary Shelley had written about. She was not very specific, but she described a man made up of other men, and we developed that idea while also creating something that was more

Below: Robert De Niro's hands, one covered by the Creature's prosthetic skin. Bottom: The make-up workshop, with several of the latex head molds for the Creature.

scientifically correct. The way our Creature's body is put together would have been medically possible in 1794—even if he could not actually have been brought to life.

"We wanted the make-up to allow the audience to feel sympathy and well as revulsion for the Creature. It's not a Monster…it's a man. So the make-up needed to be flexible enough to allow the performance to come through, but also extraordinary enough to make the audience gasp when they see it.

"During our months of research we looked at a lot of books about medical techniques of the time to find out what Frankenstein might have been able to achieve. We saw books on surgery and scars and skin disorders and wounds. We saw morticians' manuals and medical textbooks of every kind, and consulted big research establishments like the Royal College of Surgeons.

"Then we started practicing on real skin. We went to the butcher and bought pork and chicken and sewed it up to see how it would look and how different skin behaved. I don't know what the butcher must have thought we were doing…

"We did hundreds of drawings and made maquettes and slowly refined the ideas down to what we wanted. We went back and forth to New York a lot to show De Niro what we were doing and incorporated his suggestions. (At my first meeting with Ken Branagh and De Niro, I immediately attacked him and started pulling his face around. It was a good start!) He and Ken and I discussed the look at length; it was something that we all worked out together.

"Once the design was approved by everybody, we started creating test make-ups. The first step was to take a cast of De Niro's whole body, from head to toe. From that moment on, for the next eight months, he had to make sure that his body stayed exactly the same

Special Effects Make-up Designer Daniel Parker touches up the Creature's face.

shape, or the make-up would not fit properly.

"First we put a bald cap on him to get a smooth surface for the head and pasted his head and face all over with dental alinate, then plaster and a plaster bandage. When that was set, it was removed and filled with plaster to create a perfect replica of his head, with every tiny wrinkle and blemish reproduced. From this we created a master mold using silicon rubber, and from then on could take as many casts as we needed.

"The rest of his body was done section by section. We have achieved some extraordinary results with the body prosthetics for this film, many of which have never been tried before. We created a body mold that is one piece on the outside but many interconnecting pieces on the inside, like a three-dimensional jigsaw puzzle. That enabled us to get rid of the seam, which is always a problem with animatronics or prosthetics. So when you see large sections of the Creature's body—down the side, for

example—where normally there would be a seam, there is none. Just getting the molds right took months of trial and error.

"I also created an individual muscle system under the skin so you can see the muscles moving and it doesn't look like a big lump of rubber. And the hand has an individual bone system so the fingers don't look like sausages. Using the casts of De Niro, we then sculpted clay and plasticene to alter his features. Foam latex is eventually injected into the wafer-thin gap between the cast and the sculpture to create the skin that will be applied to De Niro's face and body.

"Each 'skin' has thousands of hairs, and each had to be inserted individually, using real human hairs. Each head took three to four days just to insert the hair, and a week to complete. The bodies took three weeks—and each prosthetic could be worn only once, so during the course of production we created hundreds of skins. At one time we had 50 people in the

shop working flat out.

"Robert De Niro had been closely involved in all the stages of the make-up design and preparation, so he knew what he was in for once the shooting started. On days when we had to apply the full body make-up, he would be picked up at 2:30 A.M. and be in the chair by 3:00 A.M. He would stay there, with the most incredible patience, for up to ten hours while we painstakingly glued and applied every section of skin and, when necessary, repainted it once it was on.

"The whole process was absolutely exhausting for everyone involved, but the results on screen are every-

thing I could have hoped for. It was the most difficult thing I had ever undertaken, but being asked to redesign the most famous make-up in the world puts the job into a league of its own."

Other special make-up effects executed by Parker and his team included decapitated heads, dissected corpses for anatomy lectures, an animatronic toad, plague-ridden cadavers, amputated limbs, brains and other nameless things lurking in formaldehyde. "We found this terribly skinny chap and life-casted him and then chopped it all to pieces for one of the anatomy lectures. It was done at a level of detail that could take a closeup, though none was called for on the shot.

"Strangely enough, even though I'm in special effects make-up, I'm squeamish as hell. Most of my work before this has been character and old-age make-up, not blood and guts. Show me some real blood and I'll run amok. Ask me to make several pints of it and I'm happy."

The Wrap

"I have found it! What terrified me will terrify others; and I need only describe the spectre which had haunted my midnight pillow." So Mary Shelley in her Preface to *Frankenstein* recalls her inspiration for the story, which came to her in a vivid nightmare. This most famous horror story of all time

```
DATE:Mon.Feb.7th 1994        "Mary Shelley's FRANKENSTEIN"
SHELLEY FILMS LTD                                              SHOOT DAY:67 of 81
PRODUCER:        John Veitch
CO-PRODUCERS:    Kenneth Branagh
                 David Parfitt
DIRECTOR:        Kenneth Branagh
                                             PRODUCTION OFFICE:Shepperton Studios
UNIT CALL                                    Studios Road
Rehearsal    :08.00    Director     :08.00   Shepperton, Middlesex, TW17 0QD
Ready Shoot  :08.30    D.O.P        :08.00
Lunch        :T.B.A.   Operator     :08.00   Script       :08.00
Wrap         :19.00    Asst.Cam     :08.00   Grip         :08.00   Sound        :08.00
                       1st A.D.     :08.00   Electric     :08.00   Art.Dept.    :08.00
LOCATION:              2nd A.D.     :04.30   S.P.F.X.     :08.00   Props        :08.00
C STAGE                                      M.Up/Hair    :08.00   Unit Mgr.    :08.00
                                             Costume      :05.45   Video        :06.00
                                                          :05.45   Stand Bys    :08.00
```

```
SC.NO      I/E  D/N  PGS  SET                                    CAST
Sc.179      I    N   1/8  CHALET BRIDAL SUITE                    4.
Day 40-1794                Elizabeth hears a noise and leaves the room
Sc.181      I    N   3/8  CHALET HALL                            2.4.
Day 40-1794                Elizabeth returns to her room but Creature awaits her
Sc.183      I    N   5/8  CHALET BRIDAL SUITE                    2.4.
Day 40-1794                Creature takes his revenge on Elizabeth
Sc.185pt    I    N   1/8  CHALET BRIDAL SUITE                    1.2.4.18.33.
Day 40-1794                Creatures dialogue
Sc.184      I    N   1/8  CHALET LANDING OUTSIDE SUITE           1.18.33.
Day 40-1794                The men break the door down
```

N.B. EXTREME FIRE HAZARD. ABSOLUTELY NO SMOKING ON C STAGE PLEASE

```
ARTISTE                    CHARACTER              DR.   P.Up    M.UP/W.   L.Up   ON SET
1. Kenneth Branagh         Victor                 13          
2. Robert De Niro          Creature               36    T.B.A.  07.00
4. Helena Bonham Carter    Elizabeth              34    T.B.A.  05.00            T.B.A
18.Gerard Horan            Claude                 27    05.30   06.15            10.00
33.Angus Wright            Guard 2                28    06.45   08.00            08.30
STUNTS:                                                 OT      08.00            T.B.A
Simon Crane                Co-Ordinator                                         T.B.A
Graeme Crowther            Creature Double        23                            08.00
Tracey Eddon               Double Elizabeth       18                            08.00
STAND INS:
George Asprey              for Kenneth Branagh          T.B.A                   08.00
Stephen Morphew            for Robert De Niro           T.B.A                   08.00
Joan Field                 for Helena Bonham Carter                             08.00
```

```
PROPS:
ART DEPT:      Candles, Victors pistols, Guards guns and sabres, breakaway bowl with
CAMERA:        candles and repeats.                                            08.00
VIDEO ASST:    Door to break. Canopy to tear. S/by breakaway table.           08.00
RUSHES:        As per Roger Pratt.                                             08.00
SOUND:         As per Chris Warren.
ELECTRICAL:    Screening in the Viewing Theatre T.B.A.
S.F.X.         As per Ivan Sharrock.
ARMOURER:      As per Chuck (Robert) Finch. Lightning effect
MAKE-UP/HAIR:  Practical fire, Door to break, S/by Bullet hits and window to shatter
               Richard Hooper 14.00
COSTUME:       Artistes wet. Blood on Elizabeth.
               Test on ballroom dancer, Sofia Hodges 10.00
OPTICIAN:      Artistes wet. Blood on Elizabeth.
DIALOGUE COACH Richard Glass S/by from 09.00
PROSTHETICS:   Test on ballroom dancer,
               Julia Wilson Dixon S/by from 09.30
PRODUCTION:    Creature Stage 2C. Creature wet and blood on hand. Creature stunt double.
               Motorhome for Mr De Niro parked by C Stage.
               Elizabeth's heart.
               Towels and heating to stand by for artistes.
```

```
UNIT NOTE:
1) PLEASE NOTE THAT UNIT MEMBERS MUST WEAR PASSES CLEARLY VISIBLE AT ALL TIMES.
THIS WILL BE STRICTLY ENFORCED. ANYONE WHO HAS LOST THEIR PASS SHOULD CONTACT THE
PRODUCTION OFFICE FOR A REPLACEMENT.
2) DUE TO THE COMPLEXITIES OF THE CREATURE MAKE-UP IT MAY BE NECESSARY TO SHOOT THROUGH
LUNCH. IN THIS CASE A BUFFET LUNCH WILL BE PROVIDED. THANK YOU FOR YOUR CO OPERATION.

Quote of the Day: "I was brought up to respect my elders and now I don't have to
respect anybody"
                                        George Burns
```

```
TRANSPORT
Terry Pritchard         T.B.A.    P/Up Kenneth Branagh from his home and convey to Shepperton.
Maurice Newsome         05.30     P/Up Helena Bonham Carter and convey to Shepperton.
John Hollywood          06.45     P/Up Gerard Horan from home and convey to Shepperton
Paul Grahame            T.B.A.    P/Up Robert De Niro and convey to Shepperton.
```

"haunts the imagination still," comments Kenneth Branagh. "It is one of those stories that is a combination of the simple and the profound."

Branagh and his crew wrapped up their 81 days of shooting Mary Shelley's Frankenstein right on time—81 days of the kind of intense productivity reflected in the daily "call sheet" reproduced here. It took all of that, and an even longer effort in post-production, to do justice to the power of the myth created by this twenty-year-old writer nearly two hundred years ago.

At the start of the shoot, the entire crew was presented with commemorative mugs on which were printed one of the director's favorite quotations from Shelley. In the words of Victor Frankenstein: "It was indeed a filthy process in which I was engaged...." More than once during the process, the parallel was invoked between creating a major film and creating life itself. The director, as always, has the last word: "I think Mary Shelley's story was made for this medium—it is a supremely cinematic experience."

The Undying Creature

by Leonard Wolf

In the year 2018 A.D., less than a quarter of a century away, Mary Shelley's novel *Frankenstein* will be two hundred years old. From the time it was first published in London in 1818 to the present moment, her book has never been out of print.

And yet, like Bram Stoker's later *Dracula* (1897), the Frankenstein story is better known to filmgoers than to readers. It is hard to imagine anyone old enough to go to the movies who has not been imprinted with the 1931 Universal Pictures version of Mary Shelley's story, and particularly with the image of Boris Karloff as the Creature: tall, shambling, mute, and pale with electronic pegs sticking out of his neck like a couple of quotation marks setting off a statement of pain.

In that film, his creator, Henry [the name was changed from Victor] Frankenstein, is both a baron and a doctor who, with the help of Fritz, his hunchbacked assistant, is engaged in secret research in a laboratory he has installed in a ruined mill. His goal is to recreate human life by putting together bits and pieces of anatomy gathered from corpses in graveyards and the gallows-tree. What he does not know is that he has put a criminal's brain into his creature's skull.

In the midst of a thunderstorm, Doctor Waldman, Henry's teacher, shows up at the mill accompanied by the worried Elizabeth, Henry's fiancée, and Henry's friend Victor [another name switch]. Provoked by Waldman's skepticism about his research, Frankenstein cries, "Crazy, am I? We'll see whether I'm crazy or not...."

What follows is four or five minutes of a very satisfying film sequence as the storm rages and Henry raises the gurney on which his swathed creature lies. At the climactic moment, the camera pauses over the Creature's hand and we see the trembling movement that gives Colin Clive (who plays Henry) the excuse to utter his famous line: "It's alive! It's alive!"

Dr. Waldman cautions, "You have created a monster and it will destroy you," and for a while, at least, his prophecy seems to be on target. We see how the Creature, born with its warped brain, is goaded by mistreatment to commit crime, first killing his tormentor, Fritz, then breaking loose and lurching off into the countryside, where he terrifies the populace. Everyone, that is, but little Maria, who plays sweetly with him by the shore of a beautiful lake until, in all innocence, he kills her in the very act of amusing her.

Several things make for the success of James Whale's film. First, of course, there is Whale's direction. Except for the romantic scenes involving Henry and Elizabeth, Whale attends to the details of the story with preternatural skill, alert to the smallest gestures by which people assert their humanity. Though his film is only vaguely related to Mary Shelley's novel, Whale retained its central insight: that the Creature was profoundly human, profoundly suffering, and terribly lonely.

The make-up Jack Pierce designed for Karloff is another piece of brilliance. The square home-

The EDISON
KINETOGRAM

VOL. 1   LONDON, APRIL 15, 1910   No. 1

SCENE FROM
FRANKENSTEIN
FILM No. 6604

EDISON FILMS TO BE RELEASED FROM MAY 11 TO 18 INCLUSIVE

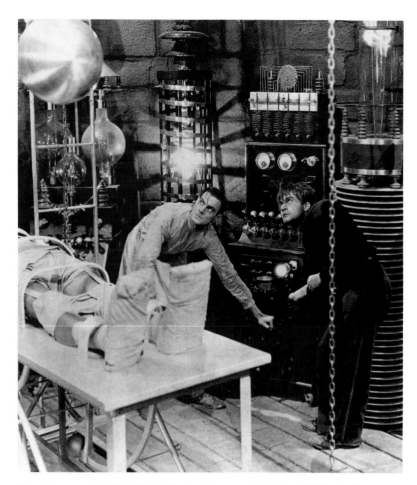

Preceding page: Left: Boris Karloff as the Creature. Right: Handbill for the first cinematic production of Frankenstein. *Above: Still from the 1931* Frankenstein: *Colin Clive as "Henry" (Victor) about to throw the switch as Dwight Frye looks on.*

made look of the face nevertheless allows us to see every delicately nuanced movement of the features. The eloquent hand motions; the invisible elevator shoes that define Karloff's shambling walk; and, of course, the electronic pegs, all combine to give us a prototypical monster—something alien from us, a thing of "show"—but at the same time the Creature's individuality, his *person*ality peers out at us from Karloff's feelingful eyes.

In 1935 Whale surpassed his triumphant *Frankenstein* with *The Bride of Frankenstein*, a film that is almost impossible to overpraise. The ingredients that make for its greatness are easy to identify: there is, again, Whale's inspired direction; there is Elsa Lanchester being delicious both as the witty Mary Shelley *and* as the bewildered, newly created Bride. As her look darts timidly from Karloff's Creature to her creator, Colin Clive's Henry Frankenstein, she leaves open the question of just whose bride she is. And of course, there is Karloff

surpassing Karloff. This time his range of emotions has been enlarged. He gets to say a few words, to laugh a little, to suffer even more deeply. As this writer noted in an earlier essay, he becomes at the film's end "one of the greatly noble, suffering victims of man's capacity to err. His Creature has all the elements of a tragic figure: dignity, decency, and more sorrow in love than anyone ought to be expected to bear."

There are two more wonderful things in this film. One of them is Ernest Thesiger playing the superbly evil and witty Dr. Pretorius, who nudges Henry Frankenstein to create the Bride. The second is the literate, marvelously paced, and poignant filmscript by William Hurlbut and John Balderston.

There have been scores of other films with the name Frankenstein in the title, some of them noteworthy. The third of the great Universal Pictures *Frankensteins* was *The Son of Frankenstein* (1939), followed by a cluster of the British Hammer Films productions: *The Curse of Frankenstein* (1957), *The Revenge of Frankenstein* (1958), *Frankenstein Created Woman* (1966), and *Frankenstein Must be Destroyed* (1969). There have been pop oddities like *Frankenhooker, I Was a Teenage Frankenstein, Abbott and Costello Meet Frankenstein*, and Andy Warhol's *Flesh for Frankenstein*; TV trivializations like "The Munsters;" and one memorable parody, Mel Brooks's *Young Frankenstein*. (See "A Selected Frankenstein Filmography" on page 186.)

But none of the films has paid much more than minimal attention to the Frankenstein story as Mary Shelley wrote it until 1994, when Kenneth Branagh, working with TriStar Pictures, made *Mary Shelley's Frankenstein*. The Branagh film, starring Branagh as Victor Frankenstein, Robert De Niro as the Creature, and Helena Bonham Carter as Elizabeth, comes closer than any film yet made in respecting Mary Shelley's story.

While reserving the right to interpret the tale in

ways that express his own sensibility, Branagh has made good use of several of Mary Shelley's themes, primarily the theme of parental responsibility. Moreover, the Creature, instead of being mute and primordial as he mostly has been in film incarnations, is literate, verbal, and sensitive, as he is in Mary Shelley. The Branagh film makes rich use, as Shelley does, of ice as a powerful symbol of various emotional failures. Best of all, *Mary Shelley's Frankenstein* gives us a Creature as triumphantly what he is: a human being, capable of reason and affection, who, as his story ends, stands before us as the prototype of suffering but dignified humanity.

~

Written in the years when the Industrial Revolution was sweeping over the world, *Frankenstein* has, through a coincidence of history, come to stand for the dangers of ever-powerful science. In our own century, when atom-splitting, genetic engineering, *in vitro* fertilization, organ transplants, and cloning have become realities, Victor Frankenstein's meddling with the secrets of life seems to resonate anew with moral overtones. As our millennium winds down, the oft-repeated cliché of science fiction films, "There are some things mankind is not permitted to know," feels more relevant than we would like to admit.

Curiously enough, though her protagonist, Victor Frankenstein, is a scientist, Mary Shelley did not write a science fiction novel. Instead, *Frankenstein* is a psychological allegory in the guise of a modified gothic romance.

The gothic romance (so-called because of the faux-medieval settings in which the stories took place: ruined abbeys, craggy castle keeps, underground vaults) is a literary genre that originated in eighteenth-century England. Horace Walpole's novel *The Castle of Otranto* (1764), usually credited with being the first of the gothic fictions, is a wooden, quirky tale that can still please an antiquarian imagination. Far better are Ann Radcliffe's

Dwight Frye as the hunchback, Fritz, unwisely provokes Boris Karloff's Creature.

Boris Karloff and Elsa Lanchester in The Bride of Frankenstein.

The Mysteries of Udolpho (1794) and Matthew
Lewis's *The Monk* (1796).

The characteristic gothic plot involved a young
woman of refined sensibility who was pursued
through bizarre, gloomy, or dangerous landscapes
by a tall dark erotically threatening man from
whom, at the story's end, she was usually saved by a
handsome, essentially uninteresting, and financially
independent young man. Typically, the gothic plot
might include supernatural (or apparently supernatural) events or objects: statues that walked, pictures that stepped down from the wall, unearthly
music or ghosts. Not infrequently the darker forms
of human behavior were touched upon: necrophilia,
incest, satanism, and other sorts of imaginative evil.

From its inception, gothic fiction was widely
read by women. More interesting still, it was
frequently written by them, so it is not at all
surprising that Mary Shelley would find Byron's
homework assignment (to write a ghost story)
congenial. What is perhaps surprising is the enduring emotional power Shelley managed to wrest
from this somewhat mannered style of fiction.
Without doubt, this power comes largely from her
ability to confront and make use of the stuff of her
nightmares—those that rose up in her imagination
as well as those that occurred in her life.

A glance at her biography, summarized at the
front of this book, is enough to reveal that personal
responsibility—particularly that of parents for children—was much on Mary Shelley's mind in the period when she conceived and wrote *Frankenstein*. Let

us look now at how those themes are developed in the novel. The story is contained in what purports to be a series of letters written by Robert Walton, a young would-be explorer to his sister, Mrs. Saville, in England. In his first letter from St. Petersburg, we learn that he is about to undertake a perilous voyage of exploration in the vicinity of the North Pole, hoping to discover a Northeast Passage. Subsequent letters from Archangel tell us that he has equipped a vessel for the voyage. There follows then an August letter informing us that his ship is icebound and his voyage of exploration on the brink of disaster.

It is at this point that he describes his encounter with Victor Frankenstein, whom Walton's sailors have rescued from the sea ice. As Letter Four ends, we get the first-person tale-within-a-tale that is Victor Frankenstein's story.

Exhausted to the very verge of death, Victor tells Walton the story of his life. We learn that he is a citizen of Geneva, Switzerland who, at age seventeen, was sent to study at the University of Ingolstadt in Germany. There, fascinated by chemistry and anatomy, he undertook certain researches that led him to the discovery of the secret of life, which then enabled him to form a living creature from assembled human parts. The creature he thus designed was eight feet tall and was intended to be beautiful. Then, "on a dreary night of November…

I beheld the accomplishment of my toils…when, by the glimmer of the half-extinguished light, I saw the dull yellow eye of the creature open; it breathed hard, and a convulsive motion agitated its limbs."

Instead of being beautiful, however, the Creature is loathsome and Victor rushes from the sight of him to his own room, where he dreams that he is embracing the worm-eaten corpse of his mother. When he wakes, it is to find the Creature beside his bed. Horrified, Victor runs away again.

And that, for a long while, is the last Victor sees of the Creature. In the ensuing months, Victor and his friend Clerval study languages. Then a letter from Geneva informs Victor that his little brother, William, has been murdered. Victor goes back to Geneva. By the time he gets there, he is convinced that William was slain by the Creature, but, despite that certainty, he remains silent when Justine, a loyal young servant of the Frankenstein family, is falsely accused and then executed for the murder.

In Volume II of the narrative, we see Victor on the Sea of Ice in the Alps above Chamounix. There he encounters his Creature, who compels Victor to listen to his (the Creature's) story—the second tale-within-a-tale. In it we learn how the Creature, abandoned by Victor, learned about the world into which he was born, fully adult and sexually mature. What is immediately clear is that the Creature is anything

Marty Feldman as "Eye-gor" in Mel Brooks's Young Frankenstein.

Undated engraving of body snatchers; the practice of robbing graves of corpses for medical use chilled the popular imagination. The Bettmann Archive.

but mute. He speaks the same sort of stilted, well-educated early nineteenth-century English prose that all the other characters in the novel speak. We are told how he acquired his education: by watching through a peephole and listening to an exiled French family in whose pigsty he has taken refuge.

At the end of his narrative, he demands that Victor, who made him oversized and loathsome, now make him a female companion. "My vices are the children of a forced solitude that I abhor," he says, "and my virtues will necessarily arise when I live in communion with an equal." Victor, after some hesitation, agrees, but the time and place of the new creation are not specified.

Meanwhile, Victor is readying himself to marry Elizabeth, his cousin, who was his companion from his earliest childhood. Oppressed by his promise to make a mate for the Creature, he delays his marriage to Elizabeth for a couple of years and goes off with Clerval on an extended tour of Europe and Great Britain.

In Scotland, Victor and Henry separate. Victor goes to the Orkney Islands, where he once more sets up what he has earlier called "a workshop of filthy creation," and there he undertakes to keep his promise to the Creature. But, just at the very moment that the female is about to come alive, Victor is overcome by revulsion and, in one of the most terrifying scenes in the novel, he tears the female apart

even as the Creature, who has been standing at the window, watches the destruction of his hopes. The despairing Creature says, "It is well. I go; but remember. I shall be with you on your wedding night."

The Creature keeps his promise and manages, many months later, to follow Victor and Elizabeth as they start their wedding journey. Outwitting the guards Victor has posted, the Creature kills Elizabeth on what would have been her wedding night.

For a considerable while after this, Mary Shelley's narrative skills falter as she seems unable to make up her mind how to end her story. Eventually she finds the direction that had eluded her, and the novel is back on track as Victor pursues the Creature into the Arctic wastes, where we see the two of them performing a strange and moving dance of recognition around each other over many months—first on land, then on the sea ice.

It is there, on the ice, that the novel—which began in the Arctic and achieved one climax in the glacial Sea of Ice above Chamounix—comes to its close. By then, the symbolic meaning of ice has been elaborated for us: ice stands for constricted feelings, for lack of responsibility, for parental indifference, for sexual coldness, for lack of generosity and, most of all, for the absence of love.

Understanding this, we understand why Mary Shelley, though perfectly willing to have Victor die

Boris Karloff as the Creature.

as the novel ends, has not written a similar death scene for the Creature. Instead, though the Creature tells Walton that he will "ascend my funeral pile triumphantly, and exult in the agony of the torturing flames…my spirit will sleep in peace…," we last see him standing "on the ice raft which lay close to the vessel. He was soon borne away by the waves, and lost in darkness and distance."

If we wonder why the "hero" of this fiction dies and the Creature lives, the answer may lie in Mary Shelley's understanding of what her story is about.

The emotional truth of her novel is embodied in that long mutual pursuit over the ice, the Creature after Victor, Victor after the Creature. What emerges in these final pages is that the novel has two protagonists: Victor, whose sense of responsibility is ambiguous at best, and the Creature, who, against overwhelming odds and with literally no help from anyone, achieves personhood. No wonder that the final phrases of this amazing fiction sound a note of triumph.

A Selected Frankenstein Filmography

by Leonard Wolf

1910   Frankenstein

A poignant first attempt to distill the Frankenstein story. Though the producer wanted to eliminate "all that was repulsive" in the original story, the face of Charles Ogle's Creature remains fairly repellent.

Producer: Thomas Edison
Director: J. Searle Dawley
Creature: Charles Ogle
Victor: Augustus Phillips
Elizabeth: Mary Fuller

1931   Frankenstein

This is the signature James Whale production that established Boris Karloff's rendition of the Creature as generations of filmgoers first knew him: tall, lurching, mute, a humanlike thing with electronic pegs sticking out of his neck. He is a horrid yet strangely sympathetic being as he reaches for light and human companionship.

Producer: Carl Laemmle
Director: James Whale
Creature: Boris Karloff
Victor (Henry): Colin Clive
Elizabeth: Mae Clarke

1935   The Bride of Frankenstein

Perhaps the most beautiful horror film ever made, it still vibrates with unforgettable characters and moments. Elsa

Christopher Lee as the Creature in The Curse of Frankenstein.

Lanchester, playing both Mary Shelley and the lightning-struck Bride, is first delicate, then dreadful. Ernest Thesiger as the supremely evil (and civilized) Dr. Pretorius is unforgettable. Boris Karloff's Creature continues to be the blasted exile from humanity whose woes (this time erotic) we mourn.

Producer: Carl Laemmle Jr.
Director: James Whale
The Creature: Boris Karloff
The Bride: Elsa Lanchester
Victor (Henry): Colin Clive
Elizabeth: Valerie Hobson

1939   Son of Frankenstein

The third of Universal Pictures' great Frankenstein series in the 1930s, this one introduces the broken-necked Ygor, played by Bela Lugosi, and the one-armed martinet police inspector Krogh, played by Lionel Atwill. The Creature, twice destroyed in the previous films, comes alive once more. The sets, more than anything else, are impressive.

Producer: Rowland V. Lee
Director: Rowland V. Lee
Creature: Boris Karloff
Baron Wolf von Frankenstein: Basil Rathbone
Inspector Krogh: Lionel Atwill
Elsa von Frankenstein: Josephine Hutchinson

1943   Frankenstein Meets the Wolf Man

Intent on mating two moneymaking themes to breed more money, Universal Pictures concocted this hybrid film. This time Bela Lugosi, who turned the part down in 1931, plays the Creature and Lon Chaney, Jr., who made the Wolf Man famous in 1941, plays that role again. There is more name recognition than talent in this film.

Producer: George Waggner
Director: Roy William Neil
Creature: Bela Lugosi
The Wolf Man: Lon Chaney, Jr.
The Mad Scientist: Lionel Atwill

1948   Abbott and Costello Meet Frankenstein

The horror-comedy is usually more funny than scary, and that's true of this film. But a lovely bunch of horror film stalwarts are gathered together here: Bela Lugosi, Lon Chaney, Jr., Vincent Price, and a whole stew of monsters: The Frankenstein Creature, Dracula, the Invisible Man, the Wolf Man. And one mustn't forget Abbott and Costello or the famous exchange in which the Wolf Man says, "You don't understand—when the moon rises, I turn into a wolf." To which Costello replies, "You and fifty million other guys."

Producer: Robert Arthur
Director: Charles T. Barton
The Creature: Glenn Strange
Sandra Mornay: Lenore Aubert
The Invisible Man: Vincent Price

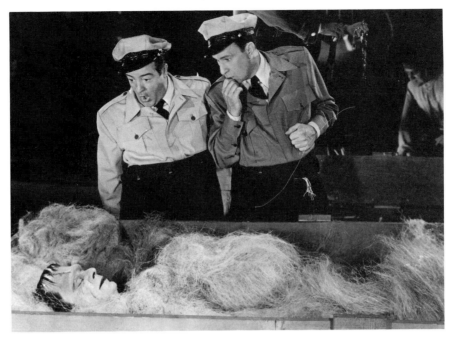

Abbott and Costello and the Creature in Abbott and Costello Meet Frankenstein.

The Wolf Man: Lon Chaney, Jr.
Dracula: Bela Lugosi

1957　The Curse of Frankenstein

This, the first of the Hammer Films, set the tone for what would turn out to be a major departure in the making of horror movies. Like its successors, *The Curse of Frankenstein* is stylish, sensuous, intelligent, and colorful. Peter Cushing is the cold, detached scientist indifferent to human suffering; Christopher Lee is the agonized Creature.

Producer: Anthony Hinds
Director: Terence Fisher
Creature: Christopher Lee
Frankenstein: Peter Cushing

1957　I Was a Teenage Frankenstein

Important only as the companion film to Herman Cohen's more successful *I Was a Teenage Werewolf* (1957) and as another in the new genre of horror films pitched specifically to a teenage audience. Here, a descendant of Victor Frankenstein, working in America, gathers body parts from accident victims to carry on his ancestor's work. The high point of the film comes when his dreadful trade is interrupted because he is eaten by a crocodile.

Producer: Herman Cohen
Director: Herbert L. Strock
Creature: Gary Conway
Frankenstein: Whit Bissell
Margaret: Phyllis Coates

1958　The Revenge of Frankenstein

A Hammer Films sequel to *The Curse of Frankenstein, The Revenge of Frankenstein* again stars Peter Cushing, this time as Baron Victor Stein, who works in a hospital ministering to the poor. Moved by the impulse to give his crippled assistant a healthy new body, he creates an artificial crea-

ture. As the film ends, the Baron, who has died, is about to have his brain transplanted into another body.

Producer: Anthony Hinds
Director: Terence Fisher
Creature: Michael Gwynn
Frankenstein: Peter Cushing
Female lead: Eunice Gayson

1966　Jesse James Meets Frankenstein's Daughter

Fans of truly bad movies treasure this one. Made as a sort of companion piece to *Billy the Kid Versus Dracula*, it has a Creature that looks as if it had been stitched together by a cobbler suffering from a hangover. But there's a certain comic and very American vitality in the fusion of the cowboy film with the Frankenstein legend.

Producer: Carrol Case
Director: William Beaudine
Creature: Cal Bolder
Frankenstein's [Grand]daughter: Narda Onyx

1970　The Horror of Frankenstein

Not one of Hammer Films' best, this is regarded by some critics as a death knell for the excellence that had come to mark that studio's horror output. Here there is a great deal of sex and violence being exploited for their own sake.

Producer: Jimmy Sangster
Director: Jimmy Sangster
Creature: David Prowse
Victor: Ralph Bates
Housekeeper: Kate O'Mara

1973　Frankenstein: The True Story
(made for television)

Notable for the first use of ice (an important thematic element in Mary Shelley's novel) in a movie interpretation, this production boasted the distinguished poet Christopher

Isherwood as a co-author of its script. Despite a spectacular beheading scene, however, the film is fairly inert.

Producer: Hunt Stromberg
Director: Jack Smight
Creature: Michael Sarazin
Female Creature: Jane Seymour
Frankenstein: Leonard Whiting
Clerval: David McCallum
Polidori: James Mason
Elizabeth: Nicola Paget

1973 Flesh for Frankenstein (Andy Warhol's Frankenstein)

As one might expect from a film to which Andy Warhol's name is attached, this is a quirky production. Phil Hardy characterizes it thus: "The action…consists mostly of copulations and disembowelings and features tons of intestines slithering in gallons of blood." There are more than a few tasteless moments as the filmmakers manipulate human flesh with very little respect for the humanity of which it was once a part.

Producer: Andrew Braunsberg
Director: Anthony Dawson (Antonio Margheriti)
Creatures: Srdjan Zelenovic and Carlo Mancini
Frankenstein: Udo Kier

1974 Young Frankenstein

The sort of movie that is called a "romp" because it is so good-humored and moves so swiftly. Much of the pleasure in watching it comes from the fact that Mel Brooks clearly loves the films and the film tradition that he is parodying. Though the macho emphasis on the Creature's outsized

Bela Lugosi, Boris Karloff, and Basil Rathbone in Son of Frankenstein.

sexual equipment is likely to make thoughtful people wince, there are enough more acceptable high jinks to sweep one along.

Producer: Michael Gruskoff
Director: Mel Brooks
Creature: Peter Boyle
Friedrich Frankenstein (pronounced "Frahnkensteen"): Gene Wilder
Blind Hermit: Gene Hackman
Ygor or Eye-Gor: Marty Feldman
Inga: Teri Garr
Elizabeth: Madeleine Kahn
Frau Blücher: Cloris Leachman

1985 The Bride

Meant as a respectful homage to *Bride of Frankenstein*, this otherwise not very exciting film has moments when one can glimpse the wonderful original.

Producer: Victor Drai
Director: Franc Roddam
Frankenstein: Sting
Creature: Clancy Brown
The Bride: Jennifer Beals

1987 Gothic

This is Ken Russell's self-indulgent and exploitative version of the famous *Frankenstein* summer of 1816, when the Byron and Shelley ménages lived near each other in Geneva. It was in Byron's Villa Diodati one rainy night that Byron assigned the task of writing a ghostly tale to his guests. But Russell, instead of developing the rich dramatic material at hand, turns this fascinating cast of real characters into a band of lunatics. No one, seeing this, would guess that Byron and Shelley rank among the world's greatest poets, or that Mary Shelley created a literary icon that still stands as an image for the dilemmas of our age.

Producer: Penny Corke
Director: Ken Russell
Byron: Gabriel Byrne
Shelley, P.: Julian Sands
Shelley, M.: Natasha Richardson
Dr. Polidori: Timothy Spall

1990 Frankenstein Unbound

Roger Corman, pioneer and master creator of memorable low-budget films, directed this adaptation of Brian Aldiss's audacious science fiction story in which a time traveler scientist is transported back to 1817 Switzerland, where he meets Victor Frankenstein and discovers that they have and/or will have similar ethical problems.

Producer: Roger Corman
Director: Roger Corman
Victor Frankenstein: Raul Julia
Mary Shelley: Bridget Fonda
The Scientist: John Hurt

Bloom, Harold. *Mary Shelley's Frankenstein*. New York: Chelsea House, 1987.

Fantasmagoriana: ou Recueil Histoires d'Apparitions. Traduit de l'allemand par un Amateur (J. B. B. Eyries). Paris: F. Schoell, 1812.

Flexner, Eleanor. *Mary Wollstonecraft: A Biography*. New York: Coward, McCann & Geoghegan, 1972.

Florescu, Radu. *In Search of Frankenstein*. New York: Warner Books, 1976.

Forry, Steven Earl. *Hideous Progenies: Dramatizations of Frankenstein from Mary Shelley to the Present*. Philadelphia: University of Pennsylvania Press, 1990.

Glut, Donald F. *The Frankenstein Catalog*. Jefferson, North Carolina: McFarland & Co., 1984.

_____. *The Frankenstein Legend: A Tribute to Mary Shelley and Boris Karloff*. Metuchen, New Jersey: Scarecrow Press, 1973.

Haining, Peter, ed. *The Frankenstein File*. London: New English Library, 1977.

Harper, Henry H., ed. *Letters of Mary W. Shelley*. 1918. Reprint. Folcroft, Pennsylvania: Folcroft Library Editions, 1972.

Holmes, Richard. *Shelley: The Pursuit*. London: Weidenfeld and Nicholson, 1974.

Jones, Frederick L., ed. *The Letters of Mary W. Shelley*. Norman: University of Oklahoma Press, 1944.

Keay, Carolyn. *Henry Fuseli*. London: Academy Editions, 1974.

Mank, Gregory W. *It's Alive!: The Classic Cinema Saga of Frankenstein*. San Diego: A. S. Barnes, 1981.

Marshall, Mrs. Julian. *The Life and Letters of Mary Wollstonecraft Shelley*. 2 vols. New York: Haskell House Publishers, Ltd., 1970.

Medwin, Thomas. *The Life of Percy Bysshe Shelley*. Introduction by J. Buxton Forman. London: Oxford University Press, Humphrey Milford, 1913.

Moers, Ellen. *Literary Women*. Garden City, New York: Doubleday & Co., Inc., 1976.

Nitchie, Elizabeth. *Mary Shelley: Author of Frankenstein*. Westport, Connecticut: Greenwood Press, 1953.

Shelley, Mary. *Frankenstein*. London: H. Dolburn & R. Bentley, 1831.

_____. *Frankenstein*. 1818. Edited by James Rieger. Indianapolis: Bobbs-Merrill, 1974.

Small, Christopher. *Mary Shelley's Frankenstein: Tracing the Myth*. Pittsburgh: University of Pittsburgh Press, 1972.

Spark, Muriel. *Child of Light*. Essex: Tower Bridge Publications, 1951.

Tropp, Martin. *Mary Shelley's Monster*. Boston: Houghton Mifflin, 1976.

Veeder, William F. *Mary Shelley and Frankenstein: The Fate of Androgeny*. Chicago: University of Chicago Press, 1986.

Walling, William A. *Mary Shelley*. New York: Tayne Publishers, 1972.

Wolf, Leonard. *The Essential Frankenstein*. New York: Plume: The Penguin Group, 1993.

The alchemist's laboratory.

Kenneth Branagh has, in his relatively brief career, established himself as among the most versatile artists currently working in film and theater, and is especially noted as an interpreter of classic literature on the screen. *Mary Shelley's Frankenstein* is the fifth major feature he has directed and starred in; the others are *Henry V* (1988), *Dead Again* (1991), *Peter's Friends* (1992), and the much-acclaimed *Much Ado About Nothing* (1993). His stage career has been equally prolific, from acting in student productions at the Royal Academy of Dramatic Art to his most recent appearances in a record-breaking run of *Hamlet* with the Royal Shakespeare Company and in *Coriolanus* at the Chichester Festival Theatre, co-produced by Chichester and his own Renaissance Theatre Company. He has also taken leading roles in many British television productions, including the series "Fortunes of War." Further details of his career are noted in the chapter "The Filmmakers and Their Creations."

Though Branagh is less well known as a writer, in addition to adapting *Henry V* and *Much Ado About Nothing* for the screen he has written two plays: *Tell Me Honestly* and *Public Enemy*, produced for Renaissance Theatre Company's first season. He is also the author of an early autobiography, *Beginning*, which raised much-needed funds for Renaissance.

David Appleby has worked as a stills photographer on movies for twenty years, after several years in the advertising industry. He views his distinguished career as a natural outgrowth of his twin passions: the cinema and photography.

Working in London in the early 1970s, a time when such directors as Alan Parker, Ridley Scott, Tony Scott, Hugh Hudson, and Adrian Lyne were making television commercials, Appleby followed them into films, shooting stills for Parker's *Bugsy Malone* and *Midnight Express*, and Ridley Scott's *The Duellists*. During this time he formed a good working relationship with producer David Puttnam, with whom he later worked on several projects including *The Killing Fields* and *The Mission*. His other credits include *Reds*, *1492*, *Mississippi Burning*, *Total Recall*, *The Commitments*, and *Brazil*.

Several of his previous assignments have been published in book form: *City of Joy*, *The Killing Fields*, *Pink Floyd: The Wall*, and two Monty Python films, *Life of Brian* and *The Meaning of Life*. When not away on locations, Appleby lives in Somerset, where he is currently compiling a book covering his twenty years in film photography.

Leonard Wolf is a multifaceted writer and literary scholar, best known for his authoritative works on terror literature and film. These include *A Dream of Dracula* (1972), *The Annotated Dracula* (1974), *The Annotated Frankenstein* (1976), *Horror: A Connoisseur's Guide to Literature and Film* (1989), and *Wolf's Complete Book of Terror*, first published in 1979 and reissued in 1994 in a new Newmarket Press edition. *The Annotated Frankenstein* was republished in softcover in 1993 as *The Essential Frankenstein*; it contains the full text of Mary Shelley's original 1818 edition as well as Wolf's illuminating introduction and notes.

Wolf is also a much-published writer of poetry, fiction, social history, and biography, and a leading translator of Yiddish literature—the finest in America, according to Irving Howe—and the designated biographer of Isaac Bashevis Singer. He has also been a professor of English, teaching creative writing and Chaucer. His writing in the horror genre has twice been honored with the Anne Radcliffe Award for Literature, and he has served as a consultant on several films, including *Bram Stoker's Dracula* and *Mary Shelley's Frankenstein*.

ACKNOWLEDGMENTS

Permission to reprint copyrighted material from the following sources is gratefully acknowledged. The publisher has made all reasonable efforts to contact copyright holders for permission; any errors in the form of credit given will be corrected in future printings.

The Bettman Archive: Page 13: Undated engraving of Geneva. Page 15: Percy Shelley's funeral, by L. E. Fournier. Page: 19: Theatre of Anatomy in Cambridge, aquatint by Combe, 1815. Page 167: Photograph of Luigi Galvani's scientific equipment. Page 180: Colin Clive and Dwight Frye in *Frankenstein* (1931). Page 181: Boris Karloff and Dwight Frye in *Frankenstein* (1931). Page 184: Undated engraving of grave robbers. Page 188: Boris Karloff, Basil Rathbone and Bela Lugosi in *Son of Frankenstein*.

Ronald V. Borst, Hollywood Movie Posters: Page 178: Boris Karloff as the Creature in *Frankenstein* (1931). Page 182: Boris Karloff and Elsa Lanchester in *The Bride of Frankenstein*. Page 183: Marty Feldman as Eye-gor in *Young Frankenstein*. Page 185: Boris Karloff as the Creature in *Frankenstein* (1931). Page 186: Christopher Lee as the Creature in *The Curse of Frankenstein*. Page 187: Bud Abbott, Lou Costello, and Boris Karloff in *Abbott and Costello Meet Frankenstein*.

John Cleare: Page 47: Alpine landscape (Mont Blanc massif). Page 104: Engraving, Vûe de la Flechère, Vallée de Chamounie by L. Weber. Collection of John Cleare. Page 113: Early morning view of Mont Blanc.

Additional Illustrations: Page 6: Woodcut by Nino Carbe for the 1932 Illustrated Editions printing of *Frankenstein*. Page 12: Portrait of Mary Shelley by Richard Rothwell, exh. 1840. Oil on canvas, 29 x 24 in. National Portrait Gallery, London. Page 14: Manuscript page from *Frankenstein*, Vol. III, reprinted from *The Annotated Frankenstein* by permission of Leonard Wolf. Page 17: Engraving by Chevalier for the 1831 edition of *Frankenstein*. Pages 171-172: Costume sketches for *Mary Shelley's Frankenstein* by James Acheson. Page 179: Announcement of the 1910 film of *Frankenstein* in *The Edison Kinetogram*, Museum of Modern Art, Film Stills Archives, New York.

We thank the following for their special contributions:

At Shelley Films, Limited: David Parfitt, David Barron, Iona Price, Lil Heyman, and especially Tamar Thomas, Assistant to Kenneth Branagh, who was our constant conduit of information and materials concerning the film. Also the creative artists in England who worked on the film and made themselves available for interviews, including James Acheson, Tim Harvey, Priscilla Johns, Daniel Parker, and Roger Pratt.

At TriStar Pictures: For their invaluable marketing and creative support, Ed Russell, Randy Smith, Jamie Geller Hawtof, Toni Berger, Dennis Higgins, Barbara Lakin, and Holly Haines; and for their administrative support, John Levy, Jon Gibson, Cassandra Barbour, and Vickie Allen.

Producers Francis Ford Coppola, Fred Fuchs, and James V. Hart, for their generous support of our book from the very start, and especially producer John Veitch, who smoothed the way for us day by day, always finding solutions to seemingly incompatible deadlines.

As ever, the dedicated and expert staffs of Walking Stick Press and Newmarket Press, especially Miriam Lewis, Jill Regan, Keith Hollaman, Joe Gannon, Caroline Urbas, and Grace Farrell. Thanks to Seth Affoumado for photographing props, and to John Cleare for his superb stock images of the Alps.

Sara Keene of Corbett & Keene Ltd., London, was an indispensable contributor, conducting most of the interviews and researching the background on which the production chapter is based.

Our deepest thanks and admiration go to David Appleby, for his moving and thrilling photographs of the making of *Mary Shelley's Frankenstein;* to the talented screenwriters Steph Lady and Frank Darabont; to Leonard Wolf, for his keen insights about Shelley's novel and the films it has inspired; and especially to Kenneth Branagh, who not only understood how to bring *Frankenstein* back to life for contemporary film audiences, but thoroughly understood and steadfastly supported this book project about it.

Esther Margolis, publisher, Newmarket Press
Diana Landau and Linda Herman, Walking Stick Press